Cool Continuum

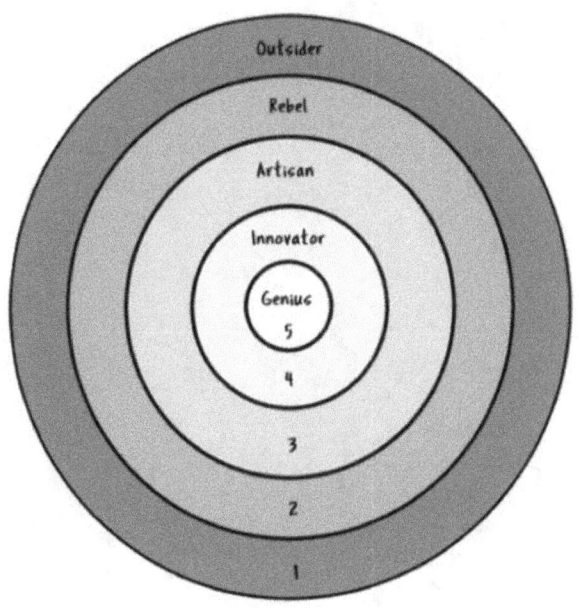

Jason S. Comely

Table of Contents

Dedication

To Kibo, Senzo, and all my pets, past and present.

Introduction

As an interdisciplinary artist, I began to ponder my own place in the world of art and what my legacy will be when I pass on (that tends to happen as you get older). Questions arose such as:

- What's a common starting point for artists, regardless of discipline?
- Can someone innovate without first mastering the art?
- Is it possible to be an artistic genius without understanding the theory?

In search of answers, the Cool Continuum was born. After many iterations of the visual model and the emergence of ChatGPT, I began publishing artist profiles online at continuum.cool. Through this, I found answers to those questions and gained even more insights. These artist profiles both serve as examples and also help define the contours of each of the five categories, which I commonly refer to as levels. ChatGPT makes it easier to provide an unbiased and balanced assessment of each artist and it sped up the writing process immensely.

This first edition you're holding in your hands is a starting point. It could use your input to take it further, to make it better. Please contribute your insights and expertise to this project at continuum.cool, and share it with your friends.

Exploring the Artistic Spectrum

The Cool Continuum is not a hierarchy. By that, I mean Level 5 is not necessarily better than Level 1. All artists on the continuum make valuable contributions. Rather than a ranking, think of it as a dynamic spectrum that recognizes the fluidity of artistic growth, pinpointing an artist's sweet spot — what I call their "natural state."

First, I'll delve into the Cool Continuum by examining its five distinct levels. Artists at Level 1, known as the 'Outsider,' lack formal training, adopt an unconventional approach to art, and face long odds for commercial success. On the opposite end, Level 5, the "Genius," consists of artists who have revolutionized their genre through mastery and flair. The intermediate levels present a fascinating array of artists, each showcasing their unique blend of musical proficiency and creative approach.

I'm also presenting a visual model of the Cool Continuum. Central to this concept is its grayscale aesthetic, which emphasizes the diversity of artistic growth and ensures the focus remains on the art itself, free from unintentional color associations. As you navigate these categories, it becomes clear that musical creation is not just black and white. Instead, it thrives on a continuum filled with varying shades of learning, evolution, and expression.

Lastly, I'll introduce over 60 artists. These profiles, written mostly by me with the help of ChatGPT, should not be seen as the final word. Like I said earlier, they are merely a starting point for conversation. I invite you to participate in this dialogue — please leave a comment at continuum.cool. Whether you agree or disagree with the perspectives shared in this book or on the blog, your contribution is valued.

Regardless of whether your passion lies in music, painting, writing, design, or film, the Cool Continuum has something for everyone. I hope you find it as engaging as I have (just maybe not as obsessively). Dive in, reflect, and discover where you might fit in this vast spectrum.

The Cool Continuum

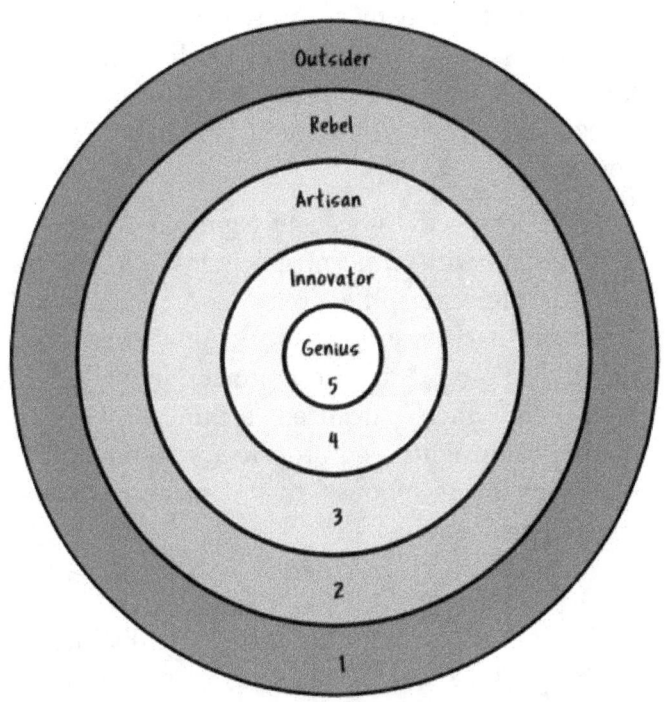

*Visual model of the Cool Continuum
by Jason S. Comely. All rights reserved.*

What you're looking at is the Cool Continuum, a new and holistic perspective on artistic expression. Not only does it categorize every kind of artist, it identifies their unique contributions across diverse domains like music, visual arts, literature, fashion, and film.

Its strength lies in capturing an artist's "natural state" — where their distinct qualities stand out and their impact is felt most. Moreover, it acknowledges that artists aren't static. Throughout their careers, they grow and evolve, potentially shifting between categories as their skills, styles, traits, and influences develop.

This perspective is visually captured using a target-like design with concentric circles. As you move towards the center, the circles become smaller. This signifies that fewer artists fit into these central categories. Artists in these inner circles are often known for their advanced technical skills, deep theoretical insights, and proprietary methods (i.e. the platforms or techniques they create or extend in transformative ways).

The Cool Continuum comprises five distinct levels: "Outsider," "Rebel," "Artisan," "Innovator," and "Genius." Each level reflects varying degrees of proficiency, understanding, and style.

Let's look at each level in detail:

Level 1 "Outsider"

Level 1 "Outsider," the largest segment on the outer rim of the continuum, captures artists who are often without formal training. They tend to explore art through the lens of other established artists or cultural movements. These individuals may be unpublished or unrecorded, but that doesn't limit their desire for self-expression and the sheer joy they find in creating.

Whether because of a lack of education or a deliberate choice to follow non-traditional routes, Outsiders are, well, outside the norm. Their work doesn't always make it to the mainstream, but when it does, it's often due to its raw, authentic qualities rather than commercial appeal.

Despite their basic grasp of traditional tools or techniques, these artists connect on an emotional level with those who feel like outsiders themselves, offering a voice to marginalized or non-mainstream audiences.

Even if most Outsiders remain relatively unknown, they still inspire those who are drawn to authentic, but unrefined, artistic expression.

Dominant character traits: uninhibited, authentic, nonconformist, empathetic, spontaneous.

Examples include: The Shaggs, Astrud Gilberto, and H.P. Lovecraft.

Level 2 "Rebel"

A Level 2 "Rebel" in the Cool Continuum is like the middle child between the untrained "Outsider" and the skilled "Artisan." While they have more know-how than Outsiders, they usually aren't as polished as Artisans. These Rebels do familiarize themselves with some basic rules, tropes, and cliches, but their main goal is to subvert them. This familiarity allows them to navigate traditional frameworks, but they're more interested in bending or breaking the rules than following them.

Rebels experiment just enough to find what they can disrupt or question. Their work is characterized by risks, which stem from a willingness to dabble in the known only to unsettle it. They're undaunted by criticism, largely because their intent isn't necessarily to improve upon established norms but to challenge them. Instead of conforming, they're committed to bucking the trend.

Their personal lives often mirror this unrestrained approach. They might lead edgy lifestyles. Their actions aren't just confined to their art; they bring these actions to life, making them tangible expressions of their philosophies.

While Level 2 Rebels might not achieve widespread success, they leave a boot mark on the art world. Their example illustrates that staying true to oneself can result in success and influence, provided one has the guts to take the leap.

Dominant character traits: defiant, unrestrained, impulsive, bold, adventurous.

Examples include: Syd Barrett, Quentin Tarantino and Hunter S. Thompson.

Level 3 "Artisan"

Level 3 "Artisan" in the Cool Continuum represents artists who start with basic skills but grow to become masters in their field. They labor diligently to develop a distinctive style that others may attempt to imitate but never quite capture. These artists also make thoughtful choices in how they present themselves and their work. Branding and perceived value are important to them.

As they improve, these artisans push their genre or medium further. They may mix unconventional elements to add complexity and depth to their creations, thereby influencing other artists across different art forms.

Although a Level 3 'Artisan' usually dedicates their life to one art form, this isn't always the case. They are recognized for their mastery, their connection with their audience, and their inspiration to future creators. The results of their craftsmanship ripple across time and various artistic fields.

In essence, these artists' work is about more than mere technical ability. It's about commitment and personal evolution. Often, they spend their entire careers honing their craft, continuously refining their work, making them true Artisans in the world of creative expression.

Dominant character traits: dedicated, persevering, disciplined, meticulous, methodical.

Examples include: B.B. King, Stephen King and Beyoncé.

Level 4 "Innovator"

Level 4 Innovators on the Cool Continuum are pioneers who "think different", as the famous Apple slogan goes. They push past usual ways of doing things and try new, creative approaches. Their work isn't just about being different; it's deeply personal and often reflects who they are. They experiment compulsively and obsessively. And it's not just people in the art world who notice — their work often becomes well-known and can even upend popular culture.

Being a Level 4 Innovator isn't about following a set path. It could be about having fun with something new, a reinvention of tradition, or finding a new way to break the rules. They're individualists with high interiority. Their work is not just a display of technique but a means of self-expression, allowing emotions, beliefs, and subconscious thoughts to manifest.

These innovators also inspire others to think creatively. They're not about quick, brilliant ideas but the result of hard work, trying new things, and taking chances. Whether it's breathing new life into old traditions or finding entirely new ways of expression, Level 4 Innovators keep the world of creativity exciting.

Dominant character traits: creative, individualistic, curious, ambitious, open-minded.

Examples include: Pablo Picasso, John Cage and Flavor Flav.

Level 5 "Genius"

At the peak of the Cool Continuum is Level 5, the spot reserved for the "Genius." The fact that this central area is the smallest within the visual model is a deliberate choice, designed to reflect how few these incredible artists truly are, and how singular they are in their abilities.

The Genius transcends conventional techniques to create profound work. They demonstrate unparalleled technical proficiency, blending mastery and creativity to redefine their respective mediums. Their work is not confined by rules; instead, they use their insights to dissolve boundaries, often collaborating with other top talent to achieve their vision.

These Geniuses connect deeply with universal themes and emotions, converting personal insights into narratives that are meaningful across cultures and time periods. They possess the ability to transform the mundane into the miraculous and make other artists better.

In essence, the Level 5 Genius on the Cool Continuum represents a rare convergence of technical mastery, creativity, universality, and lasting influence. In fields ranging from literature to painting to music and film, these artists both contribute to and define what art can be, changing the way we see the world.

Dominant character traits: insightful, intuitive, visionary, perceptive, driven.

Examples include: Miles Davis, Stan Lee, and Alfred Hitchcock.

The Rest of Us

Theoretically, there is also Level 0. It represents individuals, the "Uninitiated", who have not yet begun their creative journey or who aren't interested in making art.

The Cool Continuum is a perspective shift, another lens by which to study art and the artists that make it. Its strength lies in its subjectivity, which means you are invited to contribute your perspective to shape our collective understanding of what it takes to make art.

Enjoy the artist profiles in this book. They serve as roadmaps to artistic success, offering valuable takeaways from each artist's career. Learn what you can from these narratives and reflect on your own artistic path.

Remember, the Cool Continuum isn't just a spotlight on other artists — it's an opportunity to reflect on how you too can make your mark in the art world.

Practical Guide to the Cool Continuum

The Cool Continuum can serve as a practical guide for artists at all stages of their careers, as well as those considering diving into the arts. Here's how:

For the Aspiring Artist:

1. **Begin by Identifying Where You Stand:** Assess your dominant character traits and see if they match any specific category on the Cool Continuum. There are other important criteria to consider as well; see the 'Placing Artists on the Cool Continuum' section below.

2. **Study the Artist Profiles:** Go through the 60+ artist profiles that are available as part of the framework. Take notes on the artists who

resonate with you and that you might want to imitate.

3. **Set Your Goals:** Choose a level within the Continuum as your goal, keeping in mind the dominant traits of that category. Work backward to figure out what steps you need to take to align with or evolve into that category.

4. **Connect with Like-Minded Artists:** Find artists within the same level as you. Bond over shared traits and collaborate or seek mentorship.

For the Emerging Artist:

1. **Refine Your Craft:** At this stage, you might have gained a good grasp of your medium's basics. The next step is to focus on honing specific techniques and developing a style that sets you apart.

2. **Challenging Norms:** By now, you may be starting to experiment with your work to find new angles or interpretations. Make sure your work aligns with your identified traits, or those traits you want to develop.

3. **Personal Branding:** Observe how other artists in your category have presented their art and themselves to the world. Are you building a brand that reflects both your art and your character traits?

For the Established Artist:

1. **Redefining Boundaries:** As an Innovator or Genius, survey the lower levels for raw, untapped ideas. Sometimes, revisiting foundational traits can lead to innovation.
2. **Collaborations for Growth:** Collaborate with artists across different levels, bringing together a diverse set of traits. This fusion will either cause friction or add a fresh dimension to your art.
3. **Leave a Legacy:** Reflect on the dominant traits that brought you to your level and how you can impart these to upcoming artists. You will be shaping the future of art!

For All Artists:

1. **Regular Check-ins:** Every quarter, introspect on your dominant traits and re-evaluate your place on the Continuum. Make course corrections (if necessary) based on your self-assessment.
2. **Engage with the Community:** Initiate or participate in discussions around the Cool Continuum. Share your journey and learn from the experiences of others.
3. **Document Your Journey:** Keep an art journal or blog detailing your progression along the Continuum. What is most important is the person you are becoming, via the cultivation of new character traits.

Placing Artists on the Cool Continuum:

1. **Check the Training:** Did the artist undergo formal training or mentorship? If so, they are likely not Level 1 Outsiders, although exceptions like painter Yun Hyong-keun do exist.

2. **Innovation vs Disruption:** Differentiate between artists who innovate and those who break rules. Innovators often progress to the center of the Continuum, while disruptors are often in the Rebel or Outsider categories.

3. **Examine the Career Timeline:** Is there consistent improvement of the craft over an extended period? This suggests a move towards higher categories like Artisan or Innovator.

4. **Consider Their Achievements:** Have they achieved something widely considered impossible or extraordinary in their field? This could indicate that the artist belongs in the Genius category.

5. **Perception by Others:** Consider how the artist's work has been received by their peers, the general public, and experts in the art field.

By leveraging the Cool Continuum, you can gain insights into your creative process, identify areas for growth or change, and find a community of like-minded artists. Knowing your place on the Continuum can also assist you in positioning your art in the marketplace. For example, if you're intrigued by

Outsiders who made a significant impact, research how they managed to do so.

Remember that the Continuum isn't just for labeling where you are; it's a guide to help you figure out where you want to go. If you aim to reach a particular level, focus on cultivating its dominant traits. Also, study the profiles and books of artists in that category for inspiration and a deeper understanding of their approach to both art and life.

Syd Barrett

Syd Barrett, founding member of the iconic band Pink Floyd, was a unique bloke who broke musical conventions and helped shape the psychedelic rock genre. He stands as an archetypal 'Rebel' on the Cool Continuum.

Born as Roger Keith Barrett in 1946, he acquired the nickname "Syd" during his teenage years. Showing an early affinity for art and music, Barrett picked up the guitar at a young age and began a life of creativity. In 1965, Barrett co-founded Pink Floyd, kick-starting a journey that would see him become one of rock music's most enigmatic figures.

Barrett's approach to music was characterized by an intuitive understanding of melody and a penchant for whimsical, often abstract, lyrics. He fused these elements with an experimental use of guitar and recording techniques, creating a sound that would come to define Pink Floyd's early work. His innovative use of dissonance, feedback, and distortion painted sonic landscapes that were as unpredictable as they were compelling.

Take, for instance, the song "Interstellar Overdrive," a track from Pink Floyd's debut album, "The Piper at the Gates of Dawn." It is considered one of the first and most influential psychedelic instrumental improvisations. Its erratic tempo changes, unstructured composition, and frenzied guitar work are classic hallmarks of Barrett's "rebel" spirit.

However, being a rebel often implies a degree of resistance or defiance, and in Barrett's case, this extended to his relationship with fame. He was known for his erratic behavior and unpredictable performances, often strumming one chord for the duration of a concert or simply staring into space. This behavior, while puzzling to many, only cemented his status as a non-conformist.

By 1968, following the release of Pink Floyd's second album, Barrett's deteriorating mental health led to his departure from the band. He later went solo, releasing two albums that, while not commercially successful, further exemplified his spacey approach to songwriting and performance.

Ultimately, Syd Barrett's career was a study in unapologetic rebellion against the norms of music and society. His unique approach to guitar playing, his surrealistic lyricism, and his apparent disregard for conventional performance practices were all aspects of this rebellion. Though his career was brief and overshadowed by personal struggles, Barrett's music consistently provides a high for the listener.

Barrett's creative legacy serves as a potent reminder that, in the realm of art, it is often those who defy rather than comply who leave the most enduring impressions.

Tony Bennett

Music is like a garden, and no one took care of it quite like Tony Bennett. In the fertile fields of pop, jazz, and show tunes, he used his voice to grow songs that people have loved for many years. His ability to consistently make great music and the love for what he did places him at Level 3, the "Artisan" spot, on the Cool Continuum.

Bennett's songs aren't just performances — they are masterclasses in feeling. His soothing voice paints pictures, and captures complex emotions with the precision of a calligrapher's pen. Take "I Left My Heart in San Francisco," for example. Hear him sing it, and you can almost see and feel the city, as if you're walking its streets. That is, of course, before the escalated crime rates, drug use, and homelessness.

According to the Cool Continuum, an Artisan is an artist who really understands their craft and spends their life making it better. In his 70-plus year career, Bennett consistently demonstrated this quality, achieving technical soundness and compelling aesthetics through dedication to his craft. He was the clockmaker in the world of music — painstakingly fine-tuning each detail, treating every note as a cog in the greater machinery of his melodies.

He knew his genres inside and out, from the swing of jazz to the heartbeat of pop standards, and the dramatic crescendos of show tunes. He wasn't just a singer — he was a guide who took us on a journey through his songs.

Bennett's great understanding of music was shown in his many songs and how much respect he got from other artists. Frank Sinatra himself hailed Bennett as the "best singer in the business." This showed Bennett's commitment to his craft and how much he influenced music.

Even as music changed, Bennett kept doing his thing. He stayed true to his style instead of riding the wave of passing trends. This is what made him a perfect example of an Artisan.

Take Bennett's collaboration with Lady Gaga. The duo's album "Cheek to Cheek" bridged the generational gap, blending Bennett's classic stylings with Gaga's modern sensibilities — a demonstration of adaptability. It showed that Bennett could maintain his style while also working with new artists.

In short, Tony Bennett was a perfect example of an Artisan on the Cool Continuum. His career was more about improving over time than about making big changes. It was like a long, beautiful song that kept playing, showing us what can happen when someone truly commits to their craft.

Just like a gardener who kept taking care of his garden, Bennett took care of his music. And his garden bloomed—rich with the fruits of his Artisan labor. He showed us that music isn't always about pushing the envelope. Sometimes, it's about mastering the art of sealing it beautifully—an ode to the dedication that defines Level 3 of the Cool Continuum.

Jeff Buckley

Jeff Buckley is a singer and songwriter who enjoyed a brief career, cut short by a tragic and untimely death. However, he left a lasting impact on the music industry due to his unique and forward-thinking approach to songwriting. To this day, there aren't many artists who sound like Jeff Buckley, and few have been able to replicate the enigmatic charm of his personality and vision, let alone emulate his sound and artistry.

The son of another well-respected singer-songwriter, Tim Buckley, Jeff, was exposed to songwriting and performance at a very early age. His vocal range was impressive, influenced by classical music, even opera, and rock and folk music. In addition, Buckley's guitar skills and techniques were very sophisticated. Known for using a Fender Telecaster electric guitar, Buckley's playing was largely based on clean sounds. This sharply contrasted with the popular grunge aesthetics when he was active at the height of his career. The artist's seminal album "Grace" still stands as one of the most well-received debuts in music. Playing clean chords and arpeggio requires much more technical proficiency, as distortion can't help "mask" imperfection or create artificial sustain. This naked approach added more vulnerability to the sound of Buckley's music, and his impressive vocal technique and tone matched his guitar ability. For this reason, this artist can be placed in the Artisan level of the Cool Continuum.

In the early to mid-90s, music was undergoing some profound changes. Rock fans were moving away from the glitter and glam of hard rock. Heavy metal, the dominant form of rock music in the 1980s, was losing favor as audiences started to feel the need for a more authentic alternative. This was when styles such as grunge and post-punk music became more popular, especially thanks to artists such as Nirvana, Smashing Pumpkins, and even Green Day, among others. This new wave of rock bands was more spontaneous and favored urgency and instinct over technique and flashy arrangements.

Jeff Buckley's music stood out within these musical settings as something rather distinctive and one-of-a-kind. The artist managed to capture the spontaneity and realness that people had come to appreciate from alternative music, but without giving up on his technical mastery. Some accomplished musicians, such as The Smashing Pumpkins, almost felt they had to hide their real musicianship for fear that their skills might put alternative music fans off. However, Jeff Buckley stayed true to himself and did not try to ingratiate alt-rock fans. He showed the alternative music scene that being very proficient does not necessarily mean diluting the emotional power of music.

On the contrary, Buckley utilized his guitar skills to enhance the emotional impact of his compositions. His guitar and vocals create beautiful, melodic patterns that are as complex as passionate and expressive. "Grace" is a mesmerizing studio album that feels like a tour de force of amazing guitar textures and breathtaking vocals. Later, artists like Radiohead, Alt J, and Damien Rice expressed their deep admiration for Buckley and cited him as a prominent influence on their style. What made Buckley's legacy so important is the fact that he made a bold statement by being refined. He showed that being alternative didn't have to mean "being rough around the edges." If music comes from the heart, it doesn't matter whether it is executed by a child or with a high level of technical mastery. It's all in the emotion behind the vision.

Björk

E merging from Iceland, Björk Guðmundsdóttir, more commonly known as Björk, is a self-taught wonder. While her childhood did include attendance at an Icelandic music school, it wasn't the classical Western training many would expect. Instead, her formative years were a mishmash of choral singing, Icelandic folk traditions, and a dalliance with pop music. This blend of influences would come to serve as the fertile ground from which she cultivated her idiosyncratic and ever-evolving style.

Björk relentlessly reinvents her art. Just consider 'Biophilia,' a boundary-ignoring project that fused music, visuals, and technology into an immersive experience. This endeavor is far more than an album; it's a compelling signal of Björk's standing within the Genius level of the Cool Continuum.

Each album she crafts unfolds like a novel, with each track serving as a chapter contributing to a grand narrative. She is a master storyteller whose tales span the gamut of human emotions, universal connections, and the intricate bond between humans and nature. Her story doesn't follow a straight line but rather embarks on a multi-dimensional exploration of these themes.

Her music defies norms and exists at the intersection of pop, electronic, classical, and avant-garde—spaces where musical language mutates and evolves. Albums like "Homogenic," an electronic tapestry, and "Vespertine," a collection of whispered confessions amid frozen landscapes, offer glimpses into her sonic evolution.

Then there's "Vulnicura," an album that navigates the emotional aftermath of her breakup. More than a mere reflection, it's an invitation into her world—a chance to walk in her shoes, feel her pain, and ultimately experience her catharsis. Set against haunting strings and stuttering beats, it serves as a striking testament to human resilience.

Despite her intensely personal expressions, Björk succeeds in weaving universal narratives, cementing her unique place on the Cool Continuum. Her music does more than create soundscapes; it curates experiences, transforming passive listeners into active participants in her artistic journey.

From the versatile expressions of her voice, which ranges from gossamer whispers that float like dandelion seeds to powerful exclamations that pierce the silence, Björk's influence resonates long after the music has stopped. Her unique voice, the refusal to be confined by genre boundaries, and the ability to translate personal experiences into universal narratives all underscore her towering presence in the expansive spectrum of music.

In a landscape filled with diverse musical contributions, Björk's work continues to influence and inspire. Her distinct musical style and ceaseless innovation not only enrich the realm of music but also firmly mark her spot within the Genius level of the Cool Continuum.

Frank Black

In the sprawling mural of rock music, Black Francis, aka Frank Black, looms large, a titan straddling the gulf between punk, indie, and surf rock. His influence echoes like a power chord, from the Pixies' grimy Cambridge roots to global fame.

Starting his career in the crucible of the 80s alternative scene, Black Francis, with his unmistakable howl and distinctive songwriting, was a Level 4 "Innovator" on the Cool Continuum. A Pied Piper leading a generation of rock bands down the rabbit hole of 'loud-quiet-loud' dynamics, his stylistic fingerprints are smeared across the grunge and alternative movements.

The Pixies were the aural equivalent of Dr. Jekyll and Mr. Hyde, capable of shifting from a whisper to a wail in the blink of an eye. Their compositions bucked traditional structures, with Francis's lyrics an intricate web of cryptic metaphors and surreal imagery. Their genre-defying cocktail shook the boundaries of rock music, leaving it forever altered.

However, as Frank Black — the moniker he adopted post-Pixies — his creative energy seems to have transitioned. Black appeared to have shed his 'Innovator' skin and gracefully grown into the 'Artisan' persona — a Level 3 on the Cool Continuum. He became a musical craftsman, consciously aware of his abilities and limitations, able to apply his vast knowledge and experience to create aesthetically pleasing work.

His solo and subsequent band work were less explosive than the Pixies' sonic assaults but showed a newfound mastery of subtler, more nuanced expressions. The frantic dynamics and oblique lyrics gave way to more straightforward narratives and compositions. His songs, while no less compelling, began to hew closer to the traditional lines of rock 'n roll.

Gone were the sharp edges and frenzied vocals that characterized his Pixies era, replaced with a mellower, more polished sound. If the Pixies were a wild, untamed beast, then the later Black was a lion tamer, expertly wielding the whip and chair of songcraft.

Yet, if we were to distill his vast influence into a single point on the Cool Continuum, Level 4 "Innovator" would still seem the most fitting. His early work with the Pixies had such a profound impact on the music landscape, reshaping genres and inspiring countless artists, marking him a true disruptor in the field.

In the end, the journey of Black Francis/Frank Black isn't a tale of fading talent but a testament to his artistic evolution. From the grungy murals of the Boston music scene to the polished soundscapes of his solo work, he's proven that in the great gig of life, whether you're delivering power chords or crafted harmonies, what matters most is that you never stop playing your own tune.

Dan Brown

You probably know Dan Brown, the guy who wrote thrillers like "The Da Vinci Code" and "Angels & Demons." But did you ever think about the person behind these books? The Cool Continuum is a way to sort artists by their approach to art. From this side of the coin, Dan Brown might look like a Level 2 "Rebel."

Historically, "rebels" are those who persist in their idiosyncratic style, no matter what critics say. They do their own thing, caring more about what they want to say than what others think. If we look at Brown like this, the fit seems almost tailor-made.

Now, think about what makes a "rebel" and apply them to Brown. Defying convention? Check. Brown mixes art, history, religion, and conspiracy theories in a way that's not common or comfortable for purists and academics. It's like he's throwing everything he likes into a blender and hitting 'puree.' The result is a Dan Brown broth that's both loved and hated for its defiant flavor.

Does he stir things up? Totally. Brown's novels are less like cozy fireside reads and more like bolts of lightning, sparking controversies with their interpretations of religious symbols and historical events. He's not scared of controversy, he likes to shake things up, getting people talking.

Did he make a big impact? Absolutely. Take "The Da Vinci Code" for instance. It was more than just a bestseller. It incited curiosity, prompted debates, and even fueled tourism for its real-life locations. His work's impact spread far and wide.

Does he stick to his style, even when criticized? That's the most "rebel" thing about him. If Brown were a boat, he'd keep sailing straight, undeterred by the collision course of criticism that he inevitably encounters. He's found a storytelling style that his readers love, and he's not changing it.

So, what do you think? Does "rebel" sound right for Dan Brown? He's a writer who does things differently, shakes it up, and stands his ground, no matter how much people make fun of him.

Just like a coin has two sides, we see two sides of Dan Brown. One side is the popular author of hit books; the other side is a rebel artist. And this different look at Dan Brown isn't the final word. In fact, it's like opening a new book. Because that's the power of art — it always has more stories to tell.

Johnny Cash

To many people, Johnny Cash is practically synonymous with country music. Yet, he wasn't always considered the essential artist he is known as today. The singer-songwriter was a very unassuming performer with humble beginnings. Yet, he was able to transcend his beginnings and change the face of American songwriting in the process. His approach to music makes him an "Outsider" in the Cool Continuum, especially because he felt like an outsider and related to outsiders in society. His lyrics often delved into themes of love, heartache, redemption, and the human experience, resonating with people from all walks of life, especially those who had traveled tortuous paths.

Johnny Cash was on the underdog's side and challenged the status quo of the music industry and American society. In a time when singers aimed to project a polished and clean-cut image, he embraced a more rugged, raw, and authentic style. He wrote songs that spoke to people who felt marginalized and often overlooked. He also went to great lengths to make his music accessible to such people. Famously, Cash performed at Folsom Prison and in San Quentin in front of enthusiastic crowds of inmates who deeply appreciated Cash's vision and willingness to highlight the importance of treating all people with dignity, even criminals in jail. He was an advocate for the downtrodden and a fervent supporter of prison reform, among other causes. His music mirrored his empathy and compassion for the marginalized, as he felt like one, too, in many ways. Cash's early life was marked by hardships, including growing up during the Great Depression in a poor farming family. He also experienced many struggles in life, including substance abuse, divorce, and emotional turmoil.

Cash adopted the iconic "Man in Black" persona, wearing dark clothing on and off stage. This choice symbolized his empathy for people who were suffering and feeling left out. At the time, it was also a mind-boggling departure from what an entertainer should look like. Cash was not the typical singing star and was miles apart from the glitz and glamour of the typical music industry attire.

Known for his deeply baritone-like vocals, Cash became one of the most iconic singers of the 20th century, inspiring many generations of musicians. His range was limited, but his singing was powerful and evocative. Not only did his work inspire many country artists but also rockers and punks such as Social Distortion (Mike Ness), Bruce Springsteen, and Joe Strummer (of The Clash). Many country and rock and roll singers who were active in the 50s faded away from the mainstream, only catering to the "nostalgia markets" of music. In other words, their music didn't appeal to younger generations. This was certainly not the case for Johnny Cash, who experienced a resurgence.

Later in his career, Johnny Cash teamed up with producer Rick Rubin, who helped him achieve a musical renaissance that brought him closer to a new generation of listeners. In particular, Rubin understood that Cash was an outsider, so he paired him up with kindred spirits. He came up with the idea of Cash covering songs from other like-minded artists outside country music, and the result was astounding. From new original songs like "The Man Comes Around" to his stunning rendition of "Hurt" by Nine Inch Nails or "Personal Jesus" by Depeche Mode, it proved that Cash connected with the quintessential spirit of musical outsiders, regardless of genres or styles. Even as an 80-year-old man, Cash still had a lot to say and maintained his spirit until the very end. His resilience and coherence throughout the years added so much authenticity to his legacy, and his contribution to music and the outlaw ethos cannot be overstated.

John Cage

John Cage was a highly influential American experimental composer, known for his significant impact on 20th-century music. His artistic contributions are considered both brilliant and controversial, as the artist introduced many innovative approaches to music creation. Cage pioneered the concept of musical indeterminism, inspired by Zen aesthetics and the removal of choice from the creative process. In essence, musical indeterminism is about allowing the music to flow, surrendering to elements of chance, randomness, and unpredictability.

This approach stands in sharp contrast with the meticulous nature and tightly controlled composition frameworks used by other 20th-century composers who adhered to traditional principles. The open-ended creativity that fuels Cage's compositions is one factor that makes it difficult to categorize his work within the Cool Continuum. While he possesses traits that align with various levels, it might be helpful to examine his artistic heritage retrospectively.

Reflecting on how Cage impacted music, his radical approach transformed sound creation and the audience's experience of music in an unprecedented way. For this reason alone, Cage could be considered a Level 4 Innovator who reshaped his field, paving the way for many composers to follow. His indeterministic philosophy encouraged a departure from fixed forms and embraced a more open, dynamic approach to music writing and composition.

However, indeterminism was not the only innovative concept that Cage brought to the forefront of music. He popularized and pioneered the idea that texture is as important as melody and the notes played. In essence, it isn't just about what you play; it's also about the instrument's character and the sounds and textures it can create.

Cage carefully selected his instruments for every piece, and he took this idea even further with his concept of the "prepared piano". He would modify and rig his pianos by placing everyday objects between the strings to create unconventional sounds. He might use felt and rubber to create a soft-spoken, muted piano sound, or even springs and metal screws to produce harsher, ominous tones. Modifying instruments with household items within a classical context was considered taboo until Cage demonstrated how interesting and expressive these simple modifications could be. Many artists across various genres followed suit, giving way to a universe of possibilities. For example, the band Sonic Youth applied Cage's "prepared instruments" philosophy to their guitars, creating a new set of sounds that helped them transcend their punk roots and develop something new.

Beyond the technicalities of his compositions, Cage also focused on concept. He considered the idea behind a piece to be just as important, if not more so, than the composition itself. His affinity for conceptual art, focusing on the process and ideas behind music creation, led him to expand his work to feature multi-media installations — a novel approach for composers at the time.

One of Cage's most famous contributions to music is his unique take on silence. He believed that silence was a crucial element in his compositions, valuing the space between the notes and the silent parts of his compositions. For him, silence added drama and build-up to his pieces, and even a visual flair to performances. One of his most influential works, "4'33," consists of a pianist sitting at an instrument for the entire duration of the piece without playing a single note. The idea behind the composition is that the "silence" is not devoid of sound. Instead, it becomes an opportunity for the audience to listen to the ambient sounds in the performance space, often overlooked or considered a nuisance.

Through this, John Cage made a powerful statement: music doesn't exist in a vacuum. Each performance is intimately tied to its environment and circumstance, making for a truly unique moment each time.

Adam Clayton

A dam Clayton, the bassist of U2, can't read sheet music. This fact may surprise, even shock some. After all, Clayton's rhythms form the bedrock of U2's many hit songs, propelling them to global stardom. Yet, it's this very paradox that places Clayton squarely in the "Artisan" category of the Cool Continuum.

Clayton's bass playing has often been described as simple and even rudimentary by some critics and fans. While it's true that Clayton's bass lines lack the complexity characteristic of virtuosic players, such as Jaco Pastorius or Victor Wooten, it's this simplicity that makes Clayton an inspiring figure for aspiring musicians. His story suggests that one doesn't need to master techniques or possess prodigious talent to achieve mainstream success. Budding bassists can see in Clayton a model of attainable success.

However, it would be an oversimplification to dismiss Clayton's bass playing as basic. His simplistic approach may be a conscious choice in service of the song — a critical characteristic of the Artisan in the Cool Continuum. Clayton's bass lines are the beating pulse of U2's vibrant sound, a stable foundation upon which the rest of the band constructs its musical edifice.

It's worth noting that Clayton's minimalist approach is not necessarily indicative of a lack of ability. In fact, the discipline it takes to resist overplaying, to serve the song rather than the ego, is a mark of artistic maturity. As music producer Rick Rubin once said, "The best musicians play less." This sentiment captures the essence of Clayton's contribution to U2.

As an Artisan on the Cool Continuum, Adam Clayton demonstrates that an artist's value is not always measured by their virtuosity, but by the role they play in the broader context. Despite — or perhaps because of — his simple style, Clayton remains a pivotal member of U2 and an inspiration for average bassists who want to make it big.

John Coltrane

John Coltrane stands out as one of the most celebrated names in Jazz music. His diverse musical journey began in the US Navy, where he played clarinet and alto saxophone in a military band during World War II. After his service, he continued to play. Coltrane honed his skills in the jazz clubs of Philadelphia, often performing late into the night and participating in jam sessions with other jazz luminaries of the scene.

Even people who aren't strictly familiar with the genre might have heard of him because of his extraordinary influence even outside the jazz sphere. He quickly connected with other left-field musicians, such as Miles Davis, who pushed the boundaries of jazz with their music. The iconic saxophonist and composer fit within the "Rebel" level of The Cool Continuum for several salient reasons, especially because despite his undeniable technical skills, he opted to avoid the usual rules and standards of jazz as they were the norm at the time.

First and foremost, he lived by the concept of total musical freedom. While he was a master of his instrument, he disregarded all the rules. Instead of abiding by strict formats, Coltrane loved to improvise and experiment. His yearning for spontaneity made him stand out, especially at a time when "free Jazz" and impromptu improvisational segments were not necessarily part of the standard jazz vocabulary yet. Coltrane heavily contributed to making improvisation an integral part of modern jazz, pioneering the free jazz movement and doing away with traditional song structures and "standards." Today, this might seem like a very established notion. However, this attitude made Coltrane a true rebel during his heyday, so much so that he generated a lot of controversy for his approach. Many old-school jazz scholars were very skeptical about improvisation, as they preferred more structured and familiar jazz forms.

Unlike many other jazz musicians of his time, Coltrane was not a "clean-cut" character. He battled substance abuse issues during parts of his career, and his struggles contributed to a sense of being a rebel. Many jazz musicians were looking for steady, commercial careers as entertainers. The goal was to land a regular gig or a residency, as well as join established touring acts. Coltrane, however, had other goals. He prioritized musical growth and expression over crafting commercially viable tunes. His style made his music less accessible to mainstream audiences but encountered favor among a new generation of younger jazz musicians, who were tired of strict formats and rigid song structures.

In those years, many jazz musicians could have been described as "Artisans" in The Cool Continuum. They were preoccupied with becoming absolute masters of their craft, executing pieces to perfection. However, Coltrane, as masterful as he was, definitely opted not to place technique first. He decided instead to push the boundaries by exploring complex harmonic structures and modal improvisation, departing from the more conventional bebop and hard bop styles. Modal improvisation became extremely predominant, even outside jazz, because of Coltrane. Before him, many players would improvise based on the chords present in a given song. However, Coltrane preferred to focus on the scales, going for a more open and spacious sound that enables more freedom of improvisation to explore new ideas rather than being bound to the song's chords.

Tragically, John Coltrane's life was cut short at the age of 40 due to liver cancer caused by his lifestyle and substance abuse struggles. Despite such a tragic loss at a relatively young age, Coltrane's music lives on, and his rebel perspective continues to inspire many creatives. It's not just about jazz. Hip-hop artists like Wu-Tang Clan, Mac Miller, and A Tribe Called Quest have cited him as an influence. He also inspired electronic artists like Flying Lotus, who actually happens to be the grandnephew of jazz pianist Alice Coltrane, John's wife. His enduring legacy continues to shape the world of music and stands as a testament to a truly unconventional artist.

Miles Davis

I n the expansive world of music, certain artists stand out, not just for their talent, but for their relentless drive to redefine their field. Miles Davis, an extraordinary figure in jazz, was such an artist. His approach, far from being tethered to conventional norms, consistently pushed beyond familiar boundaries, exploring fresh ways to express the language of music.

The Cool Continuum, a classification model that rates musicians based on their musical prowess, is an appropriate context for discussing Davis's stature. Within this framework, Davis surpasses the Level 4 Innovator status, ascending to the top floor— the Level 5 Genius. To confine Davis to the role of Innovator would be to ignore the magnitude of his contribution and his place in the music landscape. Davis was not just an agent of change; he was a force that dramatically reshaped the contours of jazz.

Indeed, Davis was undeniably an innovator. He embraced change and navigated effortlessly through cool jazz, bebop, modal jazz, and jazz fusion. His distinguished body of work includes defining albums like "Kind of Blue" and "Bitches Brew". However, describing him solely as an innovator would be insufficient and overlook the full breadth and depth of his accomplishments.

The Genius designation isn't given solely for innovation, but also rewards extraordinary creativity, unmatched technical proficiency, and a distinctive, almost ineffable, additional quality. Davis wasn't just a marquee star lighting up the sky; he was the North Star, guiding a generation of musicians.

His improvisational abilities, an intoxicating blend of creativity and technique, were his 'X' factor. They could be compared to the finesse of an orator, weaving together tales on the fly, not merely by knowing the words, but by understanding their hidden depths, nuances, and resonances. Davis, too, knew his notes, scales, and chords. But more crucially, he understood the unspoken language of jazz, the sigh between the notes, the wink in the silence.

Further cementing his Genius status is his enduring legacy as a "kingmaker". His bands were crucibles of talent, the breeding ground for jazz royalty. From John Coltrane to Herbie Hancock, Davis had an uncanny knack for spotting and nurturing talent. His bands weren't just bands; they were like elite jazz finishing schools, producing musicians who would go on to carve out influential careers of their own.

In essence, Davis' genius lay not just in what he did, but also in what he ignited in others. As he famously said to saxophonist Wayne Shorter, "Don't play what's there, play what's not there." It's a Zen koan that only a master could teach, and only a fellow adventurer could understand.

In the end, it's not just about a musician hitting the right notes or creating a splash. It's about creating ripples that resonate through time, influencing others and shaping the future of the music. In this sense, Davis wasn't just playing the music, he was playing the future, swinging his trumpet like a time-traveling sorcerer.

The legacy of Miles Davis is not simply captured in albums or accolades, but imprinted on the soul of jazz itself. Another quote from Davis: "I'll play it first and tell you what it is later." True to his word, he played a symphony of a lifetime, leaving us listeners to ponder its profound significance, then, now, and forever.

Henry Darger

enry Darger was a quiet, small man who worked a humble job as a hospital custodian in Chicago, Illinois. It was only after he passed away that the world discovered the grand imaginary world he had created within his tiny apartment.

He wrote a monolithic manuscript that was 15,145 pages long. The manuscript, known as — get this: "The Story of the Vivian Girls, in What is Known as the Realms of the Unreal, of the Glandeco-Angelinian War Storm Caused by the Child Slave Rebellion," — is a labyrinth of complexity. Unlike books written by professional wordsmiths, Darger's work doesn't follow the usual rules of writing. His characters explode onto the pages with the ferocity of fireworks, while his plot lines swerve and swoop like a rollercoaster.

Darger's work is like a Baltic Wheel labyrinth, where every turn takes you deeper into its mysteries. Unlike a professional writer who carefully manages all parts of the story, Darger's work is more like an uncontrolled adventure into his psyche.

Darger never attempted to publish his work or follow popular writing trends. His creation was his refuge, a parallel universe reflecting his solitude in reality. The Vivian Girls were his fictional companions, and their fight against evil mirrored his own internal struggles. Darger wasn't just the writer of his manuscript; he was also its only intended reader.

Labeling Darger as an outsider means we value the genuine nature of his art. His work doesn't follow the usual trends or styles. His imaginary world is pure, not colonized by convention.

For Darger, writing wasn't about getting famous or leaving a legacy. It was more of an emotional catharsis. It was as though he was trying to survive on a deserted island, and his book was his message in a bottle.

Understanding Darger as an "Outsider" in the Cool Continuum helps us see a part of art that's often overlooked. His work doesn't aim to impress anyone; it's a reflection of his feelings and experiences.

In a world that often only appreciates artists with training and traditional skills, Darger's work shows us that art is also about expressing personal feelings and thoughts.

In the midst of discussing the Cool Continuum's different levels and the many types of art, we come back to Darger. His life and work may not be well-known, and it definitely differs from the mainstream, but they show us a key truth. The real value of art isn't in how well it's made or how popular it is, but in how well it expresses the artist's feelings and thoughts. In Darger's case, his work is a perfect example of outsider art — straightforward, sincere, and unforgettable.

Interestingly, Darger's work also included hundreds of drawings and watercolor paintings. Some were over 10 feet long and were designed as panoramic views of his imagined world. His art and writing complemented each other, creating a more complete picture of the Vivian Girls' adventures.

Recalling the wisdom of Kurt Vonnegut, "To practice any art, no matter how well or badly, is a way to make your soul grow. So do it." Darger, an outsider in life, did just that. He grew his soul in the solitude of his small apartment, and his words and drawings became his soul's gift to the world.

So, as we close this discussion, we circle back to its beginning, to a janitor from Chicago, who in his small room created an entire universe. His art and life, although not widely known or mainstream, provide a critical lesson: The real value of art is in its ability to express the artist's feelings and thoughts. Darger's work was sincere and unforgettable — a poignant tribute to the power of self-expression.

Bob Dylan

When it comes to music, the terrain isn't always clear cut.

Sometimes, songs don't shine through polished technique, but instead rumbles from the gut. This is precisely the brand of songwriting that is Bob Dylan, a man who shirks the glittering robes of technical virtuosity to cloak himself in the humble garb of the Rebel, level 2 of the Cool Continuum.

Bob Dylan's voice isn't a sweet serenade. It's more like a scuffed boot hitting a gravel road. It's not refined, but real. Detractors argue it's off-key, straying from traditional tonality. And they're right, of course. But the heart of music isn't neatness, it's authenticity. It's about mining the depths of human emotion, not about hitting all the right notes.

The Rebel on the Cool Continuum isn't simply a musician with rough edges. The Rebel is a rule-breaker, a boundary-pusher. Dylan embodies this spirit of defiance. His eccentric voice, his unique guitar style, his trailblazing lyrics — they all break the mold, proudly eschewing the mainstream for something more honest.

Yes, Dylan's guitar skills aren't dazzling. They're straightforward, competent, but not spectacular. But the essence of Dylan's music doesn't lie in showy riffs or intricate solos. Like a conversation with an old friend, his music connects directly, a heart-to-heart exchange uncluttered by flattery or fancy words. And that's why it works, why it stirs something deep within us.

In the grand symphony of music, if the Artisan is a well-rehearsed violinist, and the Innovator is the conductor rewriting the score, then Dylan, our Rebel, is the drummer, pounding out his own rhythm, careless of the score but in tune with the spirit of the piece. A rebel isn't about perfecting the melody, but about striking the right chord in the hearts of his listeners. And that's what Dylan does.

But where Dylan truly screams rebellion is through his lyrics. His songs aren't just music, they're powerful narratives, tales spun with a mastery that cuts straight to the bone. Using his lyrics like a painter uses a palette, Dylan splashes the canvas of our minds with vivid colors of social commentary and personal introspection. He's not just making music, he's telling stories, unveiling truths, and challenging the status quo.

Dylan doesn't just bend the rules, he breaks them, forging a path entirely his own. His award of the Nobel Prize in Literature in 2016 serves as a testament to his unorthodox journey, daring to blur the line between popular music and literature, and redefining what it means to be a songwriter.

The Cool Continuum isn't a strict ladder of achievement, but more a wide-open field, where musicians can roam free, exploring their own paths. In this vast space, technique is just one aspect of music. The essence of music is its ability to move us, and that's where Dylan plants his flag. His music, unpolished and raw, speaks directly to the human spirit.

To force Dylan into any other category would be a disservice to his legacy. He's not an Artisan, polishing every note to perfection. He's not an Innovator, reshaping the musical landscape with ground-breaking techniques. No, Dylan is a Rebel. He changed the world of music by simply being himself.

Bryan Eno

Brian Eno is an artist with a profoundly diverse background. In fact, calling him an "artist" might not adequately capture his vast contribution to culture. Eno treats music as a blend of art and self-expression. His work delves further into science and spirituality, enabling him to approach his creative endeavors from numerous angles.

Eno initially found massive success as a member of Roxy Music, a seminal band that pioneered post-punk and new-wave. Despite the band's successful run, Eno began to feel constrained. His longing for experimentation seemed to diverge from the band's direction, led by vocalist Bryan Ferry, who was interested in pursuing a more mainstream route.

Leaving Roxy Music was not a frivolous decision, but one that paid off. Being on his own allowed Eno to establish himself as a solo artist with an innovative approach to integrating rock, avant-garde, ambient music, and pop, among other styles.

Besides being an artist, Eno also excelled as a producer. His innovative approach and forward-thinking ideas brought out the best in a range of artists including David Bowie, U2, and Coldplay. With the latter, he pushed innovation to the limit, exploring the relationship between music and technology further. Eno developed a custom generative music app for Coldplay, which allowed people to contribute soundscapes to one of their songs during live concerts, even without prior musical theory knowledge or experience. Eno continued to delve into generative music, creating a series of apps with Peter Chilvers for people to download and use at their convenience. The apps allow users to create soothing ambient compositions by interacting with the controls, which do not require any musical experience. This is only one instance from a long list of interactive projects, installations, and performances Eno has curated over the years.

Eno is often credited with introducing the concept of ambient music to a wider audience. Initially, ambient was considered extremely experimental and was only popular within limited artistic circles, such as LaMonte Young's "eternal music" improvisational ensembles and drone music explorations.

However, Eno took the textures, emotiveness, and depth of ambient and successfully applied them to other genres. His classic album "Music For Airports" is often considered the beginning of contemporary new age and ambient music. According to many scholars, his innovative musical contributions are directly responsible for the rise of a unique musical niche, shoegaze, of which he is considered one of the forerunners, even though he doesn't precisely fit the genre's mold. Eno's interpretation of ambient inspired a whole generation of musicians who followed him. Unsurprisingly, Eno later collaborated with one of the genre's most influential bands, Slowdive.

The above achievements are even more remarkable considering that Brian Eno isn't formally trained in music. To this day, he doesn't know how to read or write musical notation. His approach to instruments like the piano and guitar is also unconventional, as he doesn't adhere to the "rulebook" and uses instruments as tools to create textures and soundscapes rather than merely focusing on traditional melodies. Over the course of his career, Eno transitioned from being an "Outsider" level artist to an "Innovator" on the Cool Continuum. The fusion of relentless artistic pursuit and commercial success is truly awe-inspiring, as Eno continues to set a very high standard for generations of musicians across various genres and formats.

From glam to punk, ambient, generative music, technology, mainstream pop, scores, and avant-garde, Eno's projects have consistently blurred the boundaries between genres and styles, illustrating that music isn't about categories and boxes, but an uninterrupted continuum with a spectrum that accommodates the emotional complexities of humanity.

Garth Ennis

Garth Ennis is the writer that wrote superhero comics while hating superhero comics. That might seem like a contradictory statement but such is the reality of one of the most complex and thought-provoking writers in the industry in the last thirty years.

While most comic book writers that have built their careers in Marvel and DC grew up as fans of these companies' material, that wasn't the case with Ennis. The British writer started reading war comics when he was a kid and didn't read superhero stuff until his late teens, which formed his opinion that they were "ridiculous". This would be a key aspect of his career many years down the line.

After several years doing work for companies in the UK, Ennis found his breakthrough with DC's Vertigo line, which was focused on more mature content, and took over the Hellblazer series in 1991. This series was key for Ennis, not only because he started writing for one of the most notorious comic book companies in the world, but also because he worked in this series with artist Steve Dillon, who would go on to become his partner in crime for several of his best work.

However, series such as The Preacher, which he started with Dillon in the mid-90s, showed what he was all about. This comic showed a priest searching for the Christian God as he fought several monsters along the way. One of the key aspects of the comic was Ennis' capacity for dark humor and satire, which would define his career.

Despite not liking superheroes, one of the great examples of Garth Ennis as a Rebel in the Cool Continuum is how he challenged the conventions of these characters. One huge example of this is the famed Punisher Kills the Marvel Universe miniseries that was released in 1995, which was an alternate universe where Frank Castle decides to take down the heroes one by one in gruesome fashion, showing how far Ennis' dislike of the heroes went.

While the British writer usually focused on gunmen as his main characters, as it can be shown in

his Punisher, Hitman, and The Preacher series, as of this writing, there is no denying that his most known work these days is his indie comic, The Boys.

The Boys, simply put, are Garth Ennis' "Screw you" letter to comic book superheroes.

It may sound exaggerated, but the famous adaptation, which has become a modern classic of the superhero genre, is actually fairly tamed when compared to the comic book version. Ennis had no problems showing superheroes at their absolute worst, with several characters being very obvious references to established names in Marvel and DC. Depravity of the highest order can be seen in the pages of The Boys comics, although it can also be said that Ennis sometimes goes too much for shock value, which makes the stories feel a bit too forced at times.

The importance of the series cannot be understated when analyzing Ennis' role as a Rebel in the Cool Continuum. Most comic book writers that don't like superheroes simply don't write about them. Ennis, on the other hand, went for the jugular with The Boys, to the point that it could be viewed as the ultimate critical series of the genre. Yes, it might not be as sophisticated as, say, Alan Moore's Watchmen series, but it shows a level of depravity and creative courage that most established writers wouldn't dare to do.

However, saying that Ennis is just a guy that likes hating superheroes would be doing him a disservice. He has proven time and time again that he is a very capable writer and one that can push the envelope of the medium by doing high-quality stories in genres that are not superhero-based, which is something that makes him a bit of a rarity in this industry.

Eminem

Often, we associate innovation with defiance of the status quo. In the sphere of music, it translates into novel techniques, provocative themes, and an ability to wield the baton of influence that reshapes the contours of a genre. Through this lens, the craft of Eminem — real name Marshall Mathers — unfolds as a lesson in innovation on the Cool Continuum.

Eminem's oeuvre is an audacious fusion of the personal and the universal. His lyricism acts as a mirror reflecting the harsh realities of life — from a turbulent upbringing to struggles with addiction and fame — rendered in raw, unvarnished language. This explicit self-exposure, bordering on the confessional, marked a dramatic turn in the road for mainstream hip-hop, which until then had emphasized societal narratives over personal memoirs.

His intricate storytelling talent, supported by a command over rhythm and rhyme, not only breaks but reshapes the traditional molds of rap music. Listeners found themselves drawn into his world, ensnared by his lyrical labyrinths and disarming honesty. His songs are less like traditional rap and more like lyrical narratives draped over syncopated beats, conjuring a new dimension within the genre.

The impact of Eminem's innovations extends far beyond his own success. His commercial triumphs put a magnifying glass on his techniques, inspiring a generation of artists to mimic his style and even take it to the next level. His presence and influence are felt across the musical spectrum, affixing his position as an Innovator on the Cool Continuum.

Like him or not, Eminem pushed the envelope and broadened the scope of what rap can be. The resulting massive success and influence he wields makes him an Innovator. His artistry, like a comet, blazes across the sky of hip-hop, leaving a trail for others to follow.

Flavor Flav

Flavor Flav, born William Jonathan Drayton Jr., is one of the most prominent artists in the world of hip-hop. As one of the founding members of Public Enemy, along with Chuck D, he contributed to rap music, reaching a broader audience. The group also brought social and political themes to the forefront of their music. Many rappers or hip-hop groups were not particularly outspoken in terms of politics, but Public Enemy changed all that, sparking a new generation of socially conscious hip-hop artists.

The group's lyrics often highlighted the ongoing struggles faced by African Americans due to racism and racial inequality. They shed light on the systemic injustices, police brutality, and discrimination that marginalized communities experienced. Public Enemy's outspoken lyrics made them an easy target, and the group was often the target of law enforcement, politicians and people who opposed their views. Public Enemy's outspoken stance against police brutality and racial profiling led to tension with law enforcement authorities, who often referred to them as an "anti-police" group.

Flavor Flav's role as Public Enemy's hype man and co-vocalist is one of the hallmarks of the sound of the band. He also became a fashion icon, combining glamour with streetwear, as exemplified by his signature oversized clock necklace, which is one of the most iconic hip-hop paraphernalia to this day. Despite facing personal and professional challenges, Flav's lasting impact on hip-hop and his contributions to Public Enemy's legacy remains influential to this day.

Public Enemy was known for its serious and politically charged lyrics, and Flav's humorous and lively stage presence contrasted with the group's serious tone, making him an outlier in the rap scene, showcasing that music could be extremely diverse and artists shouldn't be afraid to explore different facets of their personality. Chuck D and Flavor Flav were almost like the yin and yang of Public Enemy. Chuck D, the band's main vocalist and songwriter, was a poignant storyteller who took his role very seriously and had a lot of seriousness about his message. On the other side of the coin, Flavor Flav managed to always lighten the mood with his vibrant and colorful personality. The two sides worked really well, amplifying the group's reach and making the music more palatable in the process.

Flavor Flav's charisma and entertainment value extended beyond the hip-hop scene. His presence in popular culture, in particular his many reality television appearances, actually allowed him to reach a broader demographic, contributing to his legendary status. This talented rap icon could be described as a Level 4 "Innovator" within The Cool Continuum, especially because he took the role of the hype-man in rap to a whole new level. He wasn't just there to rile up the crowd, but he also contributed to the music with some amazing ad-libs and vocal parts, which were almost like rhythmic components, at times replacing or augmenting drum fills.

In evidence of this, Flavor Flav's voice and famous catchphrases have been sampled countless times in hip-hop and popular music. His iconic "Yeah, boy!" and other ad-libs have been frequently used in various songs, contributing to the rise of vocal sampling as a sound design technique in modern music production. Still, Flavor Flav wasn't just an ad-libs specialist. He also took the lead on various tracks, including "911 Is A Joke," an incendiary commentary on the slow (or absent) responses from emergency services and police in predominantly black communities.

Astrud Gilberto

Astrud Gilberto's music shines a light on a simple truth that's often missed in music: being a master doesn't always mean you've had formal training. The Cool Continuum, a new framework for discussing musicians, designates Gilberto as a Level 1 'Outsider'. Here's an exploration into why:

Astrud Gilberto's entrance into the music scene was anything but conventional. There were no arduous years spent in conservatories, no childhood hours dedicated to mastering scales and chords. Instead, she was a young wife swept into a recording studio, a casual encounter with destiny that let her raw, intuitive talent shine.

Her voice, tender and alluring in its simplicity, was the product not of training, but of an instinctive sense of melody. Gilberto was like a bird that sings not because it has learned how, but because that is what songbirds do. This pure, unrefined musical expression has an uncanny ability to reach out and touch listeners, bridging the gap between artist and audience in a profoundly accessible way.

Gilberto's work epitomizes the characteristics of an 'Outsider' on the Cool Continuum. Her untrained approach to music allowed her to create a signature style that was uniquely her own. The enchanting simplicity of her delivery, uncluttered by technical complexities, connected directly with her audience. She sang from the heart, and the sincerity of her performance left an indelible mark on the world of bossa nova.

In the grand scene of music, outsiders like Astrud Gilberto are like a fresh breeze. Their music comes across clear and simple, just like that breeze, and it reminds us that music isn't about showing off, but about connecting with people, stirring emotions, making us feel something. They show us that sometimes, the most beautiful music doesn't originate from training but from the untrained depth of the human soul.

Astrud Gilberto's legacy resides not just in her music but in the enduring truth she personifies: that music, at its most powerful, is just sincerity put to sound.

Lejaren Hiller

L ejaren Hiller is an American composer and music theorist, listed as a Level 1 Outsider in the Cool Continuum. He stands out for his unorthodox approach to musicianship, often exploring the many possibilities of technology and its involvement in the creative process, as opposed to approaching composition more traditionally.

Born on February 23, 1924, in New York City, Lejaren Hiller was interested in music from the start, but he also had a keen passion for technology. He discovered the then-burgeoning world of computers at a time when few could envision how computers would go on to shape the lives of virtually every human being on the planet. Hiller foresaw that computers would one day be able to contribute significantly to creative processes such as music creation and composition. To this day, Hiller is known for his groundbreaking work in computer-generated music and composition.

He was very interested in pursuing theories of indeterminacy, as well as serialism and tonality, in his compositions. These were aspects that had previously been overlooked by many traditional composers but were amplified by the growing possibilities of technology. Because of his interest in technology and groundbreaking theoretical frameworks for music compositions, Hiller stood out as an outsider in the world of modern classical music.

He played a crucial role in the electronic and computer-based music scene in the mid-20th century. Hiller also co-founded the Experimental Music Studio at the University of Illinois, Urbana-Champaign, alongside John Cage and James Beauchamp, two pioneers of avant-garde music and modern composition. This studio became a true haven for people to explore new methods of composition, particularly using electronic means and computers in non-traditional ways.

Throughout his career, Lejaren Hiller actively engaged in various computer music projects, collaborating with other composers and researchers to further push the boundaries of computer-generated music. Among Hiller's notable achievements is the composition "Illiac Suite," which he created in collaboration with Leonard Isaacson in 1957. It stands as one of the earliest examples of computer-generated music, where the Illiac I computer was employed to generate musical material using numerical and mathematical techniques.

The composition generated a huge debate in the music community and beyond. Is it still considered art if it is the work of a machine rather than the product of human creativity and intellect? While many detractors of Hiller's work have stated that some of his compositions are merely about mathematics, others have pointed out that there is a notable human element in the process. For instance, The Illiac Suite was created by a computer that selected musical elements obtained with rules chosen by a human composer. The performance of the piece itself was entrusted to human musicians. The combination of actual human performance, computer-generated scores, and human-imposed framework for the composition led to a rather one-of-a-kind scenario.

To this day, many people struggle to define Hiller's experimental approach to computer-generated music. However, his work resonated with fellow experimentalists such as John Cage. The two collaborated on HPSCHD, a suite written for 12 harpsichords and computer-generated sound tapes. This was an ambitious project, which resulted in another thought-provoking sonic experiment.

Ultimately, Hiller's lasting impact on the field solidifies his status as a pioneering figure in electronic and computer music history. He was one of the first people to explore the true potential of computers as a creative tool, always looking to push the envelope and set the bar higher in terms of what was possible. His legacy continues to inspire and challenge those in the field of music and technology.

Alfred Hitchcock

The epicenter of the Cool Continuum is reserved for the Level 5 artistic Genius who surveys their chosen domain from an unassailable vantage point. It's in this distinguished nexus that we find Alfred Hitchcock, the indisputable "Master of Suspense." Like a Panopticon — the architectural marvel designed for a singular observer to see all without being seen — Hitchcock's position on the Continuum affords him a view over all the cinematic landscape.

Much akin to the Panopticon's guard, Hitchcock holds an uncanny mastery over the cinematic domain. His command of filmmaking elements such as plot, suspense, character, and visual imagery allow him to wield an invisible but powerful influence. His every decision, every frame, every plot twist meticulously calibrated to incite the intended response from his captive audience.

Reflecting on Hitchcock's approach to storytelling, we find that he revolutionized the use of suspense in cinema. His methodology was not about revealing a surprise but delaying its revelation as long as possible, a principle evident in his films such as "Vertigo" and "Rear Window." These masterpieces are designed to create a sense of unease and anticipation that is tantamount to the feeling of being watched. Hitchcock, as the unseen observer, manipulates our emotions, dictating when we feel suspense, fear, or relief.

Hitchcock also redefined cinematic narrative with his mastery over the "MacGuffin," a plot device that drives the story but is insignificant by itself. This tool became a hallmark of his films. In "North by Northwest," the MacGuffin is a piece of microfilm containing government secrets, its actual contents never revealed. Yet, it drives the narrative, leading the protagonist on a thrilling cross-country chase. Hitchcock's diabolical genius lies in the fact that while we obsess over the MacGuffin, he's interested in the human emotions it provokes: the fear, the desperation, the relief.

The "Psycho" shower scene, one of Hitchcock's most iconic sequences, further illustrates his genius. With swift camera movements and sharp cuts, Hitchcock creates a terrifying scene without ever showing the act of violence directly. The impact comes from what he doesn't show, from the suspense he builds through the unseen and the unspoken. Again, Hitchcock as the unseen observer in the Panopticon, controls the narrative, manipulating audience emotions to create an effect far more potent than the raw depiction of violence.

Hitchcock wasn't just a filmmaker; he was an observer, a manipulator, an influencer who made Hollywood his psychological plaything. His legacy, as enduring as the Panopticon, continues to pervade the world of film, leaving no one in suspense regarding his monumental stature in the annals of film history.

Billy Idol

Punk-rock legend Billy Idol, with his platinum spikes, menacing sneer, and black leather, has long portrayed himself as a prototypical "Rebel." However, when we take a closer look, using the Cool Continuum — a framework that explores the artistic spectrum — a different, more nuanced narrative begins to emerge.

The Cool Continuum encourages us to peel back layers, to identify an artist's "natural state," where their predominant characteristics lie, and their impact is felt most acutely. While the rebel's garb fits Idol like a well-worn leather jacket, his journey and legacy in the music industry suggest his natural state might be better suited as an "Innovator."

Billy Idol's early days with Generation X placed him firmly in the "Rebel" category, a defiant punk prince on the frontlines of an insurgent musical movement. He challenged traditional norms, embodying the genre's spirit of anarchy and disestablishment. Songs like "Your Generation" and

"Ready Steady Go" embodied the ethos of punk — a middle finger to the establishment.

As Idol stepped onto the solo stage, the artist began to morph. He honed his craft, chiseling out chart-topping hits like "White Wedding" and "Eyes Without a Face." These weren't just rebellious punk anthems; they were technically sound, aesthetically compelling, and widely appealing. In essence, Idol was demonstrating a transformation, a movement away from the Rebel towards an "Artisan."

However, Billy Idol's career wasn't destined to plateau at craftsmanship. Like a punk-rock chameleon, he melded genres, fusing punk, rock, pop, and dance into a distinctive sound, painting a canvas far beyond the monochromatic palette of pure punk. He became a trailblazer in the use of music videos, realizing the nascent power of MTV before many of his peers, using it to amplify his music and carefully curated image.

Thus, Idol transformed again, this time into the Level 4 "Innovator." He revolutionized the punk genre, pushing it into mainstream recognition. The Innovator in Idol took the raw, unfiltered energy of punk and, like a skilled blacksmith, forged it into something new and influential.

Was this transformation an act of rebellion in itself? Arguably, yes. By stepping beyond the confines of pure punk, Idol rebelled against the very genre he once embodied. Yet, his rebellion served a purpose greater than just defying norms; it innovated.

Hence, while Billy Idol might don the Rebel's attire, his natural state on the Cool Continuum is within the Innovator category. His ability to blend genres, his foresight in leveraging the power of music videos, and his calculated charisma transformed punk into something palatable to the mainstream. This evolution attests to an artist whose influence stretches beyond mere rebellion.

It's fitting then, that Idol's most iconic hit, "Rebel Yell," isn't a pure punk track, but rather a genre-blending anthem with a catchy pop hook, a driving rock rhythm, and a high-energy video for the burgeoning MTV generation. It's the signature of an Innovator.

Billy Idol's journey along the Cool Continuum reminds us that rebellion is often a precursor for innovation. Beneath the spikes and leather, Idol is an innovator in disguise.

Elton John

What do Elton John and a sparkler have in common? We'll get to the answer later, but first let's talk about the undeniable talent that is Sir Elton John.

Elton John, the man who's hit piano keys more times than an over-caffeinated novelist on a deadline, is a Level 3 Artisan on the Cool Continuum. From the deeply emotive "Your Song" to the magnificent "Funeral for a Friend/Love Lies Bleeding," his piano skills are less of a performance and more of a musical magic show.

When it comes to songwriting, Elton's got the Midas touch. This isn't your average, play-it-safe kind of talent. Working with lyricist Bernie Taupin, they've cranked out classics like a pastry chef bakes croissants. From heart-wrenching ballads like "Candle in the Wind" and "Sorry Seems to Be the Hardest Word" to rock anthems that make your heart pound like "Crocodile Rock." And let's not forget "Saturday Night's Alright for Fighting," a song with a chorus that hits like a heavyweight champion. It might be the best chorus in rock 'n' roll.

Elton's been in the game for over five decades, delivering hit albums and topping the charts. And the best part? He did it while staying true to his signature style. His songs are more than catchy tunes; they're part of our collective memory, part of the playlist to our lives.

So, here's the deal. Elton John is an artisan of the highest order. He's a piano virtuoso, a skilled songwriter, and his legacy has outlasted most of his peers. He's been a shining star in the music world for decades.

Oh, and what do Elton John and a sparkler have in common? They both light up the night and make you say, "Wow." Only difference is, the sparkler fizzles out. But Elton? His music continues to shine.

B.B. King

B.B. King's place within the Cool Continuum isn't just comfortable — it's a perfect fit. And where does this titan of the blues reside? On the Artisan level, a niche that resonates with his life-long commitment to honing his craft and perfecting his guitar-playing skills.

Born in a sharecropper's cabin in Mississippi, B.B. King — Riley B. King to his parents — had a humble start in life. His musical journey began in church, where he found solace in gospel songs. From there, it was only a matter of time before the blues, with its rich textures and expressive melodies, captivated him. The challenges he faced, from poverty to discrimination, became part of his blues vocabulary. His guitar, affectionately named Lucille, was his trusted confidante and interpreter, translating his experiences into soul-stirring music.

B.B. King was an Artisan not merely because he had the talent, but because he understood his gift's essence. He recognized early on that it was not about flash or complexity, but about honesty, emotion, and authenticity. He was a master at expressing raw emotion through his strings, every note bursting with feeling.

His guitar technique, featuring beautifully composed solos that conveyed deep emotion through simple phrases, was groundbreaking. It stripped away the unnecessary, focusing instead on the core elements of blues music. His approach to the blues was characterized by a sense of restraint that highlighted the genre's core emotionality, effectively influencing countless musicians across various genres.

B.B. King wasn't just a guitarist; he was also a compelling vocalist. His voice, deep and resonant, combined with his expressive guitar work, made his performances captivating. In tracks like "The Thrill is Gone," King's guitar and voice intertwine in a conversation that transcends music, striking chords of shared human experience.

King's Artisan status within the Cool Continuum is reflected not only in his technical skill but also in his humility. Despite his fame and influence, he never considered himself above learning from others. He understood that mastery of a craft is a continuous journey of learning and exploration. His approach to music was almost meditative, a form of personal expression deeply rooted in his life experiences.

Perhaps the clearest testament to B.B. King's Artisan-level contribution to music is the legion of musicians he has influenced. Guitarists across various genres cite King as a major influence. Even after his death, his music continues to inspire, proving the timeless appeal of his artistry.

Above all, B.B. King's placement on the Cool Continuum's Artisan level is a testament to his commitment to his craft. He devoted his life to the blues, tirelessly refining his skills and always seeking to express the essence of the genre. For B.B. King, playing the blues wasn't just a job or even a career — it was a calling, and he answered it with every strum of Lucille.

As listeners, we're fortunate to have been on the receiving end of his life-long dedication to his craft. B.B. King's legacy isn't merely one of a masterful blues musician. It's a testament to the Artisan's dedication to their craft and their ability to transform their life experiences into timeless, universal music.

Stephen King

Stephen King used to clean public school toilets, a job many would flinch at, while toiling on stories that publishers showed little interest in. Today, he's a towering figure in the literary world. This transformation covers King's traverse across the Cool Continuum, reflecting his progression from an unknown writer to a figurehead in the literary world.

In his early days as a Level 1 "Outsider," King juggled jobs in a public school and commercial laundry, all the while crafting stories that did not conform to the preferences of conventional publishers. He populated his stories not with superheroes or prodigies but everyday people — schoolgirls, writers, car enthusiasts. King had a knack for seeing the terrifying potential lurking within the mundane, an "Outsider" with an unsettlingly fresh viewpoint.

As King's recognition grew, he morphed into a Level 2 "Rebel." His early novels, such as "Carrie" and "The Shining," subverted traditional horror tropes, setting the genre ablaze. King didn't pen tales of haunted castles, he introduced terror in the mundane — in high school bullying, in an isolated hotel, in the mind of a dog. This rebellious streak changed the landscape of horror literature.

As a Level 3 "Artisan," King's storytelling skill was on full display. His deep character explorations and suspense-filled narratives have not just captivated millions of readers but also become a blueprint for gripping fiction. King drilled deep into our deepest fears, relying on psychological insight rather than explicit gore.

Entering Level 4 as an "Innovator," King refreshed the genre, blending elements of horror, fantasy, and western in his "Dark Tower" series. His pioneering decision to release "Riding the Bullet" exclusively as an e-book in 2000 foresaw the digital future of publishing.

King's ascension to Level 5, the "Genius," is distinguished by more than his gargantuan influence or readership. It lies in his ability to tap into our shared nightmares, to plunge the ordinary into the terrifying. King didn't just write horror novels; he transformed his name into a synonym for literary horror. Like a black widow spider at the center of its web, King became the core of the genre, sensing every vibration, every nuance within the field.

But where does King truly belong on the Cool Continuum? Where is his "natural state"? I argue that King is most comfortably positioned at Level 3, the "Artisan." Like a skilled carpenter intimately familiar with every grain and knot of his wood, King has an uncanny understanding of the raw materials of fear and suspense. His mastery in carving out believable characters, weaving intricate plots, and eliciting primal emotions firmly roots him in the artisanal level. Here's where King's work glows, where his impact is felt the strongest.

In Stephen King's traversal through the Cool Continuum, we see an artist's evolution from an "Outsider" to a "Genius". His artistic metamorphosis has profoundly impacted both literature and cinema. From cleaning school toilets to sitting on the throne of literary achievement, King's story, rather than instilling fear, provides an inspiring lesson we can all learn from.

Gladys Knight

Gladys Knight, a prominent figure in Motown and soul music, is widely considered one of the most iconic R&B vocalists. During the late 1960s and early 1970s, she fronted Gladys Knight and the Pips. This was actually a family music group from Atlanta, GA, but it captivated audiences worldwide. Family groups were rather popular in those years, but the Pips experienced a massive level of popularity, particularly due to Gladys' unique vocal style and ability to lead the ensemble. The band received many accolades and achieved significant milestones over nearly 40 years of recording and tours. The group even scored a number-one hit with "Midnight Train to Georgia," released in 1973.

As someone who spent the vast majority of her life in the music business, Gladys Knight stands out as a great example of the artisan level in The Cool Continuum. She is incredibly gifted and spent many years honing her craft. Still, the music industry can be demanding. With pressures to maintain success, uphold deals with record labels, and navigate the ups and downs of a career, tensions might fall into place. This eventually led the family band to call it quits after a long and successful career. This was truly the end of an era for Gladys, but she was determined to reinvent herself.

Following the Pips' permanent hiatus, Gladys embarked on a solo career, closing out the 80s with her well-received single, "License To Kill." The track was part of the soundtrack to a James Bond movie, and it is still widely considered to be one of the best "Bond songs" of all time. The movie featured allowed the artist to reach an even broader following and continue to experiment with her musical choices. Her album, "Good Woman," was a great example of her willingness to further refine her sound.

While the singer stayed true to her roots, she also expanded her formula, demonstrating her ability to keep up with current trends and expand her sonic vocabulary. Additionally, Gladys Knight also recorded many songs that ventured into the gospel genre. As a fervent believer and member of the Church of Jesus Christ of Latter-day Saints, she took many opportunities to record faith-based music that highlighted her religious side. The artist also collaborated with many of the most influential talents in soul, gospel, and R&B, including Babyface and Patty LaBelle, only to mention a few.

Even the many cover songs she recorded received consistent praise, showcasing her Artisan qualities as a performer and arranger. She had a talent for interpreting songs and infusing them with her own unique style. Her natural charm and confidence on stage and in the studio drew audiences in, and she was always able to connect with her audience on an emotional level. Many singers have notable vocal techniques, and others have pure empathy in their singing style. Gladys Knight was blessed to have both. She had the perfect combination of singing prowess and emotional power, which are two key elements of her soulful style. Her ability to infuse passion and authenticity into her performances set her apart as a truly gifted vocalist.

With such a storied and diverse career, it is not surprising that Gladys Knight earned her title as "Empress of Soul," a warm tribute to her influence and contribution to the industry.

Rupi Kaur

Today's world of poetry has a relatively new platform, and it's social media. Rupi Kaur, with her plain-spoken approach, leads the way down this unconventional path. According to the Cool Continuum, she's a stellar example of a Level 1 "Outsider."

Kaur didn't get famous through the glossy pages of literary magazines, but on the digital plains of Instagram. Instagram is a Wild West with no set rules, no guards at the gate. Kaur taught herself how to write poetry and used Instagram as a space to share her work with others.

Kaur's poetic technique, characteristically direct and accessible, is a marked departure from the dense and complex works often associated with the literary elite. As Kaur herself puts it, "I am the product of all the ancestors getting together and deciding these stories need to be told." Some people in the poetry world think her work is too simple and lacks style. But her clear, stripped-down writing is exactly what you'd expect from an Outsider in the Cool Continuum: an artist who, depending on whom you ask, may lack proficiency but compensates with raw creativity and a yearning for self-expression and instant feedback.

Another thing that makes Kaur an Outsider is just how name-recognizable she is for a poet. But Kaur's poems are easy to get. They're about things that people can relate to. Her writing is the literary equivalent of comfort food when it's not jarring you with its intensely personal subject matter. It speaks directly to the hearts of her readers, many of whom are young, social-media-savvy individuals who may not otherwise engage with poetry. In providing an entry point for this demographic, Kaur has effectively expanded the traditional boundaries of the poetry audience.

Finally, the biggest reason Kaur is an Outsider is because she's made noise in a world that's usually quiet like a library. The establishment, used to controlling the conversation about what constitutes "real" poetry, has found itself shaken. Kaur has proven that poetry need not be cryptic to be meaningful, and that a digital platform can be just as influential, if not more so, than a hardbound collection on a bookstore shelf.

You might think that because Kaur's books sell so well, she can't be an Outsider. However, within the framework of the Cool Continuum, commercial success does not necessarily equate to a shift in category. Even though lots of people know her name, those who've been in the poetry world for a long time still see her as an anomaly, her nontraditional route and style setting her apart.

Rupi Kaur, an Outsider on the Cool Continuum, is like a star that doesn't fit in any of the known constellations in the sky. Her raw, clear style, and the new audience she's brought to poetry all contribute to her unique position. Her influence is particularly notable in how she has "democratised poetry and literature in general" — again, her words. In a sense, she's created her own constellation. Looking up to Rupi Kaur through the magnifying lens of the Cool Continuum, it's clear that there are other ways to get your poetry out there.

Kraftwerk

B ack in the 1970s, electronic music was seen as a matter of curiosity. Electronic composers weren't taken seriously as an alternative to "real musicians" by most people, especially in the pop and rock realm. Many people considered synthesizers as novelty instruments and failed to realize just how powerful and groundbreaking these tools could be. As the name suggests, a synthesizer could indeed synthesize, i.e., emulate, and recreate an approximation of pretty much any type of sound or instrument. With a single synth, one could replace a full band with enough knowledge and creativity. German outfit Kraftwerk showed the world exactly what could be done, using synths not as a colorful addition to their music but as the main centerpiece and its driving force. For these reasons, they could be described as Innovators in the Cool Continuum.

Formed in Düsseldorf in the early 1970s, the band had a futuristic mindset right from the get-go. The band's original line-up featured Ralf Hütter, Florian Schneider, Karl Bartos, and Wolfgang Flür, all contributing to the artistic vision to several degrees of involvement.

Hütter and Schneider, in particular, stood out as the driving force behind the band's vision. Under their meticulous artistic guidance, Kraftwerk established a unique fusion of electronic rhythms, minimalist aesthetics, and visuals that were inspired by sci-fi.

Kraftwerk's breakthrough came in 1974 with the release of their album "Autobahn," an ambitious suite that showcased the immense potential of synthesizers in modern music. Inspired by Germany's highway system, the song was a real milestone moment in the history of music. By that point in time, many people had never heard synthesizers, let alone vocoders, with the ability to transform the human voice into a robotic set of harmonies. Following releases, such as "The Man-Machine" (1978) and "Computer World" (1981), continued to push the boundaries of electronic music.

Initially, the band's sound could be described as proto-synth-pop. However, the group eventually focused on the dance-friendly component of their sound with more emphasis on rhythmic elements. For this reason, many people consider them pioneers and precursors of techno and house music. Kraftwerk's music often featured repetitive rhythms, ostinatos, and minimalist compositions, creating a hypnotic and trance-like quality. These techniques would later become the basis of many electronic dance music styles. Even Detroit techno pioneers like Juan Atkins, Derrick May, and Kevin Saunderson have openly acknowledged the influence of Kraftwerk on their music, highlighting their significant importance on the global music scene.

Kraftwerk's music often explored futuristic themes, from technology and automation to the impact of modernity on society. This sci-fi-inspired approach is still a very prominent trope in electronic music. Even massive artists such as Daft Punk and ILLENIUM have later embraced similar aesthetics, taking the concept to new mainstream heights.

Some critics argue that Kraftwerk's use of vocoders and robotic vocal delivery can lead to a lack of emotional depth in their music. However, this was an intentional choice to further intensify the sense of futurism in their music, and it was a subtle commentary on the increasingly blurred relationship between man and machine, which the group anticipated with quasi-prophetic foresight.

Kraftwerk's music is such a critical influence on electronica that people can actually still hear them on many modern tracks. Many of their synth chords, drum hits, and other elements have been sampled to the point that most producers using them might not even know where the sounds originated from!

Scott LaFaro

In the realm of jazz, where improvisational innovation is the lifeblood of the genre, LaFaro's contributions shine. With his groundbreaking bass style, his compositional acumen, and his aptitude for reshaping the role of the bass, LaFaro fulfills his calling as a Level 4 Innovator on the Cool Continuum.

LaFaro's bass style is nothing short of revolutionary. His virtuosic performance and fearless exploration of the instrument's capabilities pushed the boundaries of what was deemed possible on the double bass. Nowhere is this more evident than in the seminal live recording, "Sunday at the Village Vanguard," featuring the Bill Evans Trio. In this album, LaFaro's contrapuntal bass lines intricately interweave melodic tapestries, engaging in a captivating dance with Evans' piano and Paul Motian's drums.

Contrapuntal, a term often associated with classical music, assumes a renewed vitality in LaFaro's hands. His bass becomes an agile conversationalist, engaging in musical dialogues that transcend traditional accompaniment. Like a gracious host mingling amongst guests, he interacts with the other musicians, interjecting, supporting, even challenging. The bass, no longer confined to its subservient role, emerges as a melodious force, an equal partner in the trio's musical conversations. LaFaro's contrapuntal bass style becomes a metaphorical tightrope walker, gracefully navigating the interstices between the piano and drums. His bass playing is impossible to ignore.

Beyond his bold bass playing, LaFaro's two compositions provide testament to his creative mojo: "Gloria's Step" and "Jade Visions." These original works, exquisite tunes performed by the Bill Evans Trio, showcase LaFaro's dexterity as both a bassist and a composer.

Even in his short life that was cut tragically short, Scott LaFaro still embodies the spirit of artistic reinvention. He liberated the bass from its traditional supporting role, transforming it into an expressive force that demanded attention. In doing so, LaFaro not only left an impact on the jazz world but also changed jazz trio dynamics forever.

Rob Liefeld

Rob Liefeld is one of the most successful and controversial figures in the world of comics. Although he has been a significant figure in the industry, boasting some of the best-selling issues in the medium's history, creating household names like Cable and Deadpool for Marvel Comics, and being one of the founders of Image Comics in the early 90s, he remains one of the most debated figures in the industry's history.

Robert Liefeld grew up as a huge fan of Marvel Comics, with series such as the X-Men being personal favorites of his. In that vein, as he matured, he began to draw and practice sequential storytelling on his own, developing his style, albeit one that still required refinement.

By the mid-80s, Rob had entered the conventions circuit in the industry, showcasing his samples to a variety of Marvel and DC professionals in the hope that they would offer him a chance. He managed to catch the attention of industry stalwarts like Mike Zeck, Jim

Shooter, Marv Wolfman, George Perez, and many more. Eventually, Liefeld was given a chance at DC Comics with a few issues of Hawk & Dove, but it would be his work with Marvel Comics in the late 80s that made him a household name.

In 1989, Marvel chose Liefeld to be the new penciller for the series The New Mutants in issue #86, an X-Men spinoff. The series, then written by Louise Simonson, wasn't selling particularly well, so it was viewed as a chance for Rob to gain experience and make his mark. However, his dynamic and action-based art propelled the title to unprecedented heights, becoming one of the highest-selling titles in the industry. A significant highlight for him was the debut of Cable in that issue, a character who would become one of the most popular X-Men characters in the 90s.

By issue #98, Liefeld had also become a co-writer with a new collaborator, Fabian Nicieza, and revamped The New Mutants into X-Force, a series with a greater focus on action and visual impact. In fact, issue #98 also marked the first appearance of Deadpool, making it one of the most sought-after comics in the medium's history.

However, due to dissatisfaction with Marvel's treatment of its freelancers and the lack of rights over their creations, Rob and six other artists, including Todd McFarlane, left the company to form Image Comics in 1992. This new publisher granted 100% rights to the creators of each comic, a move that significantly changed the industry and motivated creators to produce their work.

The first-ever Image comic was the debut issue of Liefeld's own title, Youngblood, which featured a superhero team that was also incredibly rich and famous. It became one of the best-selling comics of all time, solidifying Rob's status as a comic book rockstar, with appearances on the Dennis Miller Show and a spot in a Levi commercial.

Despite his notoriety, Liefeld often faced criticism for his artwork and storytelling abilities. Critics frequently ridiculed him for his characters' lack of proportion, misunderstanding of sequential storytelling, inability to draw feet, and an overemphasis on action without sufficient story to support it.

All these criticisms are fundamentally accurate, and it's also acknowledged that he was a self-taught artist who reached the top of his industry. This positions Rob Liefeld as a rarified Level 1 Outsider in the Cool Continuum. Despite his perceived deficits, Liefeld understood his audience and helped pave the way for a revolution in the comic book world in the early 90s, an upheaval that perhaps hasn't been replicated in the medium ever since.

Therefore, while there is much valid criticism of his work, there is no denying that Liefeld is a great example of an outsider who gave maximum effort and made a maximum impact.

Lil Wayne

L il Wayne is undoubtedly one of the most polarizing characters within the contemporary rap community. Some people consider him one of the greatest rappers of all time, while others despise him and regard him as a talentless hack. Regardless of personal opinions and feelings, it's undeniable that Lil Wayne made a massive impact on the rap world, inspiring generations of artists and paving the way for modern "trap" music as we know it. Rising to prominence in the early 2000s as part of the rap group Hot Boys, Wayne quickly established himself as a solo artist, delivering a string of critically acclaimed albums.

One of the main reasons Lil Wayne is a Level 1 "Outsider" on the Cool Continuum is that he achieved his success and status despite a lack of musical training. He doesn't play any instrument (although he dabbles in rudimentary guitar playing) and doesn't even sit down to write his music. The rapper has repeatedly claimed that he does not write any of his lyrics down. Instead, he prefers to let the moment inspire him. In the studio, Lil Wayne would always stand in front of a mic in the booth, setting the mood and letting the engineer roll the tape. He would rap on the spot and eventually select the best bits and pieces from his improvisations to form the backbone of his songs and lyrics. This process highlights the purely instinctive nature of Lil Wayne's artistry, which is essentially a visceral emotional response. He doesn't book studio time with a plan. Instead, he lets things happen and goes with the flow.

The studio experience is extremely relaxed for Lil Wayne, but the studio isn't the only environment where the iconic rapper marches to the beat of his own drum. The artist has angered crowds and promoters by showing up ostentatiously late at shows, often canceling on a whim minutes before massive performances in front of thousands of fans are supposed to take place. This attitude might be seen as unstable and erratic, but it's also another side effect of Lil Wayne's need for absolute freedom with his creativity and approach to music. As an outsider he doesn't really make art. In a way, he "is" the art. His entire attitude, lifestyle, and approach to being a rapper are like a genuine, impromptu performance with uninterrupted flow. It doesn't matter whether he's rapping, being interviewed, or playing a live show. It always feels like Lil Wayne is being himself 100% of the time.

This natural, effortless charisma makes him an outsider, as he often beats the odds without even trying. Still, acting without any restraint can have its side effects. There's a price to pay for complete freedom, and at times, Lil Wayne's career and life have experienced some bumps in the road, including several run-ins with the law and some jail time. Despite personal struggles and legal issues, Lil Wayne is still going strong. Many rap fans view him as a symbol of resilience, constantly reinventing himself and leaving an indelible legacy even with no background or significant lyrical dexterity compared to peers such as Jay Z, Kanye West, or Kendrick Lamar. Wayne might not have the articulation and poise of the artists mentioned above, but he certainly has the heart and soul to make up for it.

Another sign of Lil Wayne's natural penchant for not following rules and being boxed in is his vocal passion for music, regardless of genre definitions and other aesthetic limitations. While his sound falls within the broader descriptor of hip-hop music, Lil Wayne is a self-described rock fan with a huge passion for Nirvana, Metallica, and Blink-182, even going as far as touring and collaborating on music with the latter.

Maud Lewis

The life of Maud Lewis was colored by hardship. She lived with birth deformities and later developed severe rheumatoid arthritis. Yet, these physical limitations could not confine her imagination and desire to create. She started painting Christmas cards with her husband, and soon her creative talents bloomed like the wildflowers that graced her art.

In an isolated one-room house that she transformed into her canvas, Lewis conjured scenes of rural life with a sense of joy and simplicity. Her subjects ranged from horse-drawn sleighs to hummingbirds, and were brought to life with bright, primary colors. While the formal art world was occupied with abstract expressionism and pop art, Lewis remained unswayed, faithfully capturing her immediate surroundings with childlike wonder.

Her works were not rooted in artistic theory, nor did they yearn for intellectual interpretations. Yet, they possessed an unpretentious charm that resonated with many. Lewis's art broke through socio-economic barriers, reaching a wide audience, with her works even finding their way into the White House during Richard Nixon's presidency. However, this was not a journey from obscurity to fame for Lewis; she continued to live her modest life, selling paintings from her home, never caught up in the whirlwind of the art market.

Critics often point to Lewis's lack of formal training, noting the absence of perspective and the two-dimensional portrayal of her subjects. But such criticisms miss the heart of what makes Lewis an 'Outsider'. She was not bound by classical norms, and her art was unfiltered, unmarketable, and unaltered by academic influences.

Lewis's paintings, teeming with life, contrasted sharply with her isolated existence, illuminating her extraordinary ability to extract joy from hardship. Her artistic journey was a silent rebellion against her physical constraints and socio-economic status. Her influence now extends far beyond the confines of her tiny painted house, inspiring a new generation of artists and art enthusiasts.

Maud Lewis's categorization as an "Outsider"on the Cool Continuum is indisputable. She reminds us that art, in its most authentic form, is a reflection of life as perceived by the artist, irrespective of formal training or recognition. Her works are like lesser-known attractions in the big metropolis of art, secret places that draw their charm not from the towering skyscrapers or the glittering lights of mainstream acclaim, but from the cul-de-sacs of personal experience and a boundless imagination.

Thus, the story of Maud Lewis asserts that artistry is not solely the province of those sequestered in elite academies. It also blossoms in the least expected places, prevailing by a passion for creation. The story of this incredible woman's life and art provides an important viewpoint — it shows us that frequently, the most captivating and interesting stories are those that aren't in the spotlight or on the main stage.

Jack Kirby

When we think of the stories and characters that Marvel has given us throughout history, most people associate it with a name: Stan Lee. However, Lee's work on a creative level was not as important as it was in the advertising and media side of things. In the purely artistic area, Jack Kirby is considerably more recognized for his work in the creation of some of the most iconic characters in history such as Thor, Captain America or the Fantastic Four. Not for nothing did he come to be nicknamed The King!

Using the Cool Continuum — a framework that explores the artistic spectrum — we are going to define Kirby as an artist within the categories established in this criteria. Born Jacob Kurtzberg, he had many pseudonyms throughout his career such as Jack Curtiss, Curt Davis, Lance Kirby, Charles Nicholas and obviously Jack Kirby, with whom he became known. In the early 1940s, he teamed up with Joe Simon and capitalizing on their patriotism along with a time when

World War II defined the world, they created Captain America for Timely Comics.

A character who, wearing the colors of the American flag, confronted Adolf Hitler, in a war context, something that could almost be considered advertising for army recruitment, but which over the years evolved to become one of the most important superheroes in history. It's a smattering of Kirby's innovativeness that made him fit within level 4 of the Cool Continuum scale.

Kirby's comics career was interrupted by his involvement in the war, and by the time he returned, he found that Timely Comics was slowly losing the prominence it had during World War II. After a few years without a defined direction and almost on the verge of bankruptcy, Kirby joined Stan Lee and they began to work together on many characters and stories that would mark the future of comics and even cinema. From that union, the Fantastic Four or Thor would come out, as well as works such as the Galactus Saga.

The dynamic between the two artists was particular since Lee was the scriptwriter and raised general ideas while Kirby materialized them according to his vision and gave the stories a more solid form, hence we have particularities such as the birth of the Silver Surfer, who didn't appear in Stan Lee's original script, but Kirby included it, thus leading to the creation of one of Marvel's most iconic characters. That's just a small example of Kirby's creative nature and prolific contribution to the world of comics as well as his evolution to Genius status, Cool Continuum level 5.

For reasons that have never been made entirely clear, Kirby left Marvel for DC Comics, where far from lowering the bar or tarnishing his legacy, he created comics like New Gods, Mister Miracle, Forever People and Superman's Pal Jimmy Olsen and then what would become a crossover of those four stories that he would call The Fourth World, a concept that dealt with the confrontation of two worlds, one called Apokolips, led by Darkseid, a tyrant who was in search of the Anti-Life Equation and the other, New Genesis, led by Orion, the son of Darkseid, who had been raised by Highfather Izaya.

The King was a creative talent from the beginning of his career that we could classify as a level 4 due to his innovative ideas and concepts that had not been seen. However, time catapulted him to level 5 for his outsized output and the ability to bring crude and general ideas to works of art that are recognized even to this day. I think that's what ultimately defines Kirby: he's an artist whose work will stand the test of time.

H.P. Lovecraft

Picture a lighthouse standing solitary against a gloomy sky. There's a guy inside, writing stories that make your skin crawl and your eyes widen. He's H.P. Lovecraft, an artist shrouded in mystery.

Reading Lovecraft's stories is like taking a walk on an alien planet. Each one is stranger than the last, and they all have a certain chilling quality, just like the life of the guy who wrote them.

His writing style is dense and arcane, not everyone's cup of herbal tea. Like a song full of weird chords that don't quite go together, his stories stick with you long after you've read them. But back in his day, not many people were interested in his tales of cosmic horror.

To top it off, his stories were riddled with xenophobia, reflecting his personal prejudices. These unfortunate views made him even more of an outsider, pushing him further away from the mainstream crowd. Lovecraft was the quintessential outsider, going against the norm, creating work as weird and complicated as he was.

Reading a Lovecraft story is like getting lost in a maze. His stories don't follow a predictable path; they twist and turn, descending into the shadowy corners of the human mind. He wasn't trying to sell you a nice, neat story; he was leading you into your own darkness.

His creation — the Cthulhu Mythos — still resonates with a niche audience, which has embraced Lovecraft's intricate lore and expanded on his universe in exciting ways. But his influence remains an acquired taste, a whispered secret shared among a dedicated few rather than a household staple. Like the signature scrawls of an eccentric artist, Lovecraft's tales are for those who seek the scary.

However, in the depths of his stories lurked a darker, more disturbing current. His writings mirrored his personal beliefs, tinged with a racism that was unfortunately prevalent in his time. This fact pushes Lovecraft further into the realm of the literary outsider.

Was Lovecraft a misunderstood genius or a man condemned by his personal flaws and unconventional style? The answer is as layered as the man himself. Nevertheless, to cast him as an "Outsider" on the Cool Continuum doesn't downplay his skill but underscores his individuality. Lovecraft, the lighthouse keeper, shines a beam of idiosyncratic creation into the murky waters. His ghost in the annals of horror sends shivers down the spine of convention, a reminder that artists need not bend to the whims of the crowd.

By placing Lovecraft in the "Outsider" category, we aren't making an apology for his flaws but acknowledging his raw creativity that flourished despite them. And isn't that the essence of an "Outsider"? They exist on the fringe, thriving in their isolation, boldly expressing themselves despite the odds.

So, as the Lovecraftian fog lifts, we see him standing against the storm, a solitary figure on the outer edges of the Cool Continuum. Lovecraft, the outsider, challenges our perception of art, forcing us to peer into the abyss and confront the monsters that lurk within. His legacy, as turbulent as the seas of his cosmic horrors, serves as a stark reminder that sometimes, we scare ourselves the most.

Bobby McFerrin

T here are artists whose voices stand out, not just for the melodies they produce but for the groundbreaking ways they manipulate sound. Bobby McFerrin, the acclaimed American vocalist and conductor, is one such artist. With his unique vocal techniques, he not only blurs but leaps over genre boundaries, effortlessly balancing between the worlds of jazz, classical, folk, and pop music.

Listen to McFerrin's discography, and you're in for a treat, a meander through a garden of aural delights that seem implausible from a single voice. From his chart-topping hit "Don't Worry, Be Happy" to the daring vocal improvisations on albums like "Spontaneous Inventions," McFerrin's work doesn't just walk the path less traveled — it blazes a trail through uncharted territory.

Positioned within the Cool Continuum, McFerrin comfortably sits as a Level 4 "Innovator." It's not that he's 'higher' or 'superior' to others on the Continuum, it's simply a testament to his boundless ingenuity. The

"Innovator" label is for those artists who paint outside the lines of musical norms, who turn the canvas upside down and sideways, creating art that redefines how we perceive music.

Take a deep dive into McFerrin's most renowned piece, "Don't Worry, Be Happy." It's not just a song — it's a statement, a musical manifesto demonstrating that a song doesn't require traditional instruments to reach the top of the charts. Instead, it relies solely on McFerrin's voice and body percussion, generating all the instrumental sounds and creating a sonic illusion of a one-man band.

His innovation extends beyond his own performances. McFerrin has fearlessly navigated multiple genres, collaborating with world-renowned orchestras, demonstrating his ability to adapt and innovate within the structured world of classical music. It's this fearless crossing of boundaries that earns him a spot among the Innovators.

Yet, for all his innovation, McFerrin remains accessible. His performances of crowd favorites, like Bach's "Ave Maria," accompanied by audience participation, create a bridge between the performer and listener. This balance between innovation and accessibility is part of what makes his place on the Cool Continuum so remarkable. He doesn't just push the boundaries — he invites the audience to come along for the ride.

Digging into McFerrin's work is akin to entering a sonic labyrinth. You never know where the next turn will take you. Will it be an unexpected jazz riff? A classical interpretation? An improvised vocal spectacle that turns the concert hall into a playground of sound? It's this unpredictability, this commitment to continuous exploration, that truly defines McFerrin's place on the Cool Continuum.

Of course, describing McFerrin's musical prowess is a bit like trying to describe a sunset with a handful of grey shades — it's beautiful, but the words barely scratch the surface. To truly appreciate his contributions, you need to hear him. So tune in, take a moment, and allow yourself to be swept away by the innovative artistry of Bobby McFerrin. You'll soon see why he resonates so profoundly within the Innovator level of the Cool Continuum.

Todd McFarlane

Todd McFarlane is arguably one of the most successful comic book creators after Stan Lee, with an impressive career that stands out even more given his dedication to drawing.

The Canadian artist was born in 1961 and, like most people, became a comic book fan. However, his commitment to his craft made him an Artisan in the Cool Conundrum early on. You see, most creative people only do what they like and don't put in the leg work to get themselves out there and grow as professionals, but McFarlane did, and that proved to be the key to his success.

According to the man himself, he sent over one hundred samples per month in the early 80s to comic book publishers to see if they would be interested in his work. As he was being rejected and learning from the letters he received from the publishers, McFarlane would work every week on a specific body part to improve his anatomy art and learn more about how movement in comics works.

After a couple of runs at DC Comics and working on two issues of the Batman: Year Two story, McFarlane moved to Marvel Comics. One of his most important works there was the Incredible Hulk run he had with writer Peter David. In fact, if it wasn't for this run, perhaps none of what happened later would be a reality today.

McFarlane defined the Gray Hulk design that made such an impact during the early stages of David's run in 1987 and 1988, with the issue of the battle between the aforementioned character and Wolverine being one of the most celebrated in McFarlane's career. His attention to detail, his unique style, and approach to storytelling made him one of the most interesting young artists at the time.

However, his success would become even more prominent when he became the artist for The Amazing Spider-Man comics. It's no secret that Spider-Man is one of the most important characters in comic book history: even our grandmothers know a fair share about Spider-Man.

Therefore, when McFarlane took over the title as an artist, it was strange to see that the character was stuck in a rut.

Now, this doesn't mean that the character wasn't having great stories. On the contrary, he was doing very well. However, the art had become a bit stagnant. It seemed that most artists were just copying what John Romita did in the early 70s. So, McFarlane decided to add his own approach to the character, and it revitalized the title.

The results were amazing (pun intended), with Spider-Man sales going through the roof and Venom, a character he created along with writer David Michelinie, becoming one of the most important in Marvel's roster of villains in the coming years. Todd even got his own Spider-Man series that was a commercial success, although he received criticism for the story.

However, by the time the early 90s arrived, Todd McFarlane, Rob Liefeld, and five other major artists at Marvel realized something: they were responsible for the vast majority of these sales and were not receiving a lot of the profit. Sure, the royalty checks were great, but compared to the whole influx of money, they seemed like little. McFarlane had very little control over characters he created, such as Venom. Therefore, they decided to make a major decision.

McFarlane and the other six artists left Marvel in 1991 and formed Image Comics, a company where each creator would own 100% of their comics' rights. Todd was the most outspoken about it, which often led to controversy with other creators. Regardless, the stage was set and McFarlane delivered what is arguably his most important achievement: Spawn.

Spawn was released in 1992 and became one of the highest-selling indie comics of all time. McFarlane's art with the character has become iconic and he, now a man who understood the business side of things, managed to take Spawn to movies, video games, animated series, and a lot more. It has managed to become a very successful brand, including the massive success McFarlane has had in the toy industry.

Even today, McFarlane continues to work on Spawn. With the series now exceeding three hundred issues and McFarlane's own wealth reaching millions, he's the epitome of an artisan, having achieved it all while mastering his craft.

Sinéad O'Connor

Not many artists have shaped their own story like Sinéad O'Connor. On the Cool Continuum, she's clearly a "Rebel". Her strong refusal to go along with the crowd, her bravery in expressing her beliefs, and her special musical skills place her in a group that doesn't always follow the rules.

The Dublin-born singer burst into public consciousness with her 1990 cover of Prince's "Nothing Compares 2 U". Her voice, devastatingly raw and heartbreakingly tender, cut through the airwaves, offering a depth of emotion seldom heard before. She didn't just cover Prince's song, she claimed it as her own. But it wasn't just her powerful, tear-soaked vocals that got everyone's attention. It was also her brave vulnerability. This quality led her into a rebellion where only a few artists dare to go.

Reflecting on her infamous Saturday Night Live performance in 1992, O'Connor once said, "It's not as important to me that I'm understood as it is that I'm heard." Indeed, heard she was. After delivering a haunting a cappella rendition of Bob Marley's "War", she held up a photograph of Pope John Paul II, tore it into pieces, and declared "Fight the real enemy". It was a profound statement against the Catholic Church's handling of child abuse cases, an issue deeply personal to her.

O'Connor's rebellion permeated her music too. Her refusal to adhere to pop music conventions defined her sound. Her compositions dived into the depths of her soul and resurfaced with songs that shimmered with authenticity. She wielded her musical talent like a sword, slicing through societal expectations to reveal her truth.

Her lyrics, too, echoed her fighting spirit. The 1994 single "Famine" is a stark example. It's a fervent denouncement of the way Irish history, specifically the Great Famine, has been portrayed. Her use of lyrical storytelling as a tool of rebellion was as potent as her public acts of defiance.

As journalist Barney Hoskyns once remarked, "O'Connor was never afraid to face the storms of controversy. Her honesty and courage were her guide, leading her through the tempests of public opinion."

Her fearless approach to life and music won her many fans. Her acts of rebellion spoke to those who wanted something real in a world that often hides behind a mask. In many ways, her rebellion was her shield, her tool, and her song — a melody that reached out to those who were willing to listen and to really hear.

In the world of the Cool Continuum's view of artistic expression, Sinéad O'Connor was a fighter, a bright light among the ever-changing pressures of what society and the music industry expect. Her story, full of daring and rebellion, fits within the framework of the Continuum, showing us what it really means to be a "Rebel" in the vast world of art.

Her breath may have left her body, but her spirit and her message live on. Looking back on O'Connor, her friend and fellow artist Peter Gabriel said, "She moved to her own beat, no matter how out of sync it might have seemed to the world. In her dance, she was, and still is, a strong example of the power of rebellion." And in the world of the Cool Continuum, that's the beat we remember, the rhythm of a true level 2 "Rebel" that will continue to inspire and cajole us.

Yoko Ono

Yoko Ono is a Japanese multimedia artist and musician who currently resides in New York City. Her work spans art, music, and filmmaking, with a focus on conceptual and performance art, as well as social activism. A profound influence on the modern avant-garde movement, Yoko gained global recognition for her collaboration with John Lennon of The Beatles. Their artistic partnership culminated in timeless songs and a strong message of peace, which had an impact on a global scale. Throughout her life, Yoko Ono has championed human rights, environmental preservation, and gender equality, among other causes. Fearlessly challenging norms and conventions, the artist continues to inspire generations with her unique vision, based on promoting love, understanding, and a better world for all.

In spite of her positive intent, many people show a lot of resentment towards Yoko Ono, primarily because she is often blamed as a main factor behind The Beatles breaking up. Even after the tragic death of

John Lennon, the surviving members of The Beatles have stated that Ono has been blamed unfairly. In many ways, her work has been overshadowed by her involvement with the "Fab Four."

Yoko Ono is an Outsider within The Cool Continuum because, despite facing so much backlash and controversy, she stayed true to her artistry and concepts. Prior to her involvement with John Lennon, Ono actually worked with composers John Cage and LaMonte Young, as she was particularly interested in the Fluxes art movement. Some of these influences actually ended up leading The Beatles to open up about experimenting with their music and sound design, going where not many bands had gone before in the studio. It is not a stretch to say that Yoko Ono played a large part in making experimental music more accessible, given her influence on The Beatles and Lennon and their huge popularity, which made it more widespread. Later generations of artists, including Sonic Youth, My Bloody Valentine, and Elvis Costello, have all recognized her "unsung hero" contribution to the global music scene.

As a musician, Yoko Ono brought a philosophical twist to her work, often channeling her inner intuition and instincts in unique ways. Yoko Ono was very knowledgeable about philosophy, and her art was heavily influenced by Swiss thinker and psychoanalyst Carl Jung, among others. In her music, she often tapped into the depths of the collective unconscious, exploring themes of primal emotions, dreams, and the subconscious.

In addition, Yoko Ono's collaborations with John Lennon, such as the albums "Double Fantasy" and "Milk and Honey," can be seen as an exploration of the transformative power of love and the integration of both masculine and feminine aspects, which are among the most important themes in Jungian psychology. Some of Ono's best work transcended musical styles and focused on capturing feelings. Her album "Season Of Glass," a visceral response to Lennon's murder, is a prime example. The Japanese performer went on to collaborate with some of the world's most notable musical artists, including Peter Gabriel and Ornette Coleman, as well as new groups such as Tuneyards and her son Julian Lennon. She has explored countless genres and styles while retaining her core values.

Ono's work was driven by very precise concepts, and many people fail to realize the deep intellectual exploration that is often at the core of her works. While Ono's skills aren't traditionally what one would expect from a musician, she brought a whole new set of abilities to music, showing that a philosophical concept and thought-provoking attitude could be just as valid as years of musical education. Her legacy continues to challenge and inspire, demonstrating that music and art can be vehicles for profound philosophical inquiry and social change.

Donny Osmond

In the mercurial world of music, few figures have a track record that matches Donny Osmond's. Much like a triathlon athlete, he's successfully transitioned from being in a rock-pop band to co-hosting a variety show with his sister Marie, even shining on Broadway stages. And he's not finished yet. With a career spanning over half a century, Osmond is an ideal Level 3 "Artisan" in the Cool Continuum.

The seed of Osmond's career was planted in a devoutly religious household, as a member of the Church of Jesus Christ of Latter-day Saints. In hindsight, this path was not a roadblock but a guiding compass, directing his creative decisions even as he skyrocketed to fame at an early age with his siblings in The Osmonds.

The young star's course altered with the release of his solo hit, "Puppy Love." This song not only propelled him into public recognition but also clinched him as a distinct voice in the music industry. A voice that, intriguingly, provided a striking counterpoint to the boisterous anthems of defiance that were commonplace in his era. Amid a scene saturated with 'sex, drugs, and rock 'n roll,' Donny presented an alternative — an entertainer who stuck staunchly to a family-friendly persona.

His unyielding commitment to his values didn't seem to limit him. Instead, it carved out a niche, amassing a legion of fans drawn to his constancy and artistry. His career didn't just survive; it flourished.

An unexpected duality emerged within this artisan label. Osmond's rigid adherence to his morals presented such a stark contrast to his peers that it painted him as a rebel of sorts. Ironically, his rebellion was rooted not in defiance, but in faith.

Even Ozzy Osbourne, the notorious Prince of Darkness, found himself drawn to the paradox that was Donny Osmond. He declared 'Crazy Horses,' an Osmond chart-climber, one of his favorite rock songs. A surprising connection between these seemingly disparate artists.

Donny Osmond's career, characterized by longevity, loyalty to his religion, and an acute self-awareness, is more than a series of paradoxes. His knack for reinvention and unearthing new outlets for his talents speaks to his enduring spirit. The Artisan isn't defined by their influence on the landscape but by their survival within it. Osmond's refusal to bow to industry standards, his relentless pursuit of authenticity, and his ability to adapt have seen him maintain relevance over six decades.

Given his resilience in an ever-fluctuating industry, Donny Osmond certainly fits the mold of a true Artisan — steadfast, dedicated, and astoundingly adaptable.

Jackson Pollock

Jackson Pollock defied expectations and transformed the world of painting like a roaring natural force. With a career that contributed to the development of abstract expressionism, Pollock personifies the idea of a creative maverick and is firmly positioned as a Level 4 "Innovator" on the Creative Continuum.

Pollock's artistic journey was rooted with early exposure to diverse influences, from Native American culture in his Wyoming hometown to his study of American mural painting under Thomas Hart Benton in New York. These experiences ignited his passion for painting, forming the bedrock of his significant contribution to abstract expressionism. As he navigated the stormy currents of the art world, Pollock's career was expedited by his many experiments and bulldog-like tenacity.

The creation of Pollock's well-known drip painting technique marked a turning point in his artistic career. He embraced the unexpected, giving up the typical canvas easel in favor of laying his canvases on the ground. This new approach allowed him to realize his artistic potential. In a mesmerizing waltz of dripping, pouring, and splattering paint, Pollock's artworks burst forth, revealing the essence of his thoughts and emotions.

Pollock's paintings attracted onlookers because of their kaleidoscope of colors and dramatic arrangements. The observer was drawn into a visceral experience as each brushstroke and drip evoked a feeling of motion and spontaneity. These works of art, including the well-known "№5, 1948" and "Autumn Rhythm (Number 30)," continue to stand as timeless examples of Pollock's creative brilliance.

Through speculation and interpretation through a psychoanalytic lens, Pollock's distinctive painting style and the spontaneous, expressive quality of his works have opened up new insights into his subconscious and emotional states. Some art experts and psychiatrists believe that Pollock's drip paintings, with their compositions that seem chaotic and uncontrolled, are a reflection of his inner self. Similar to the psychoanalytic technique of free association, the act of pouring, splattering, and dripping paint onto the canvas may be perceived as a cathartic release. Pollock's actual feelings and ideas seem to have flowed onto the canvas as if his subconscious mind had taken over, controlling his hand and directing it.

To be clear, Pollock didn't invent the drip-splatter technique — the method has roots in diverse cultures

— but it was Pollock who transformed it into a distinctive, large-scale form of spontaneous expression, intricately connected with his own subconscious. This innovative approach, coupled with the enigmatic aura surrounding his process, solidified his reputation in the art world and made the drip painting technique synonymous with his name.

It's impossible to overstate the significance of Pollock's contributions. He broke through the barriers of creative convention as a leader of the abstract expressionist movement, opening the door for future generations of artists. The art world felt liberated by Pollock's bold investigation of form and gesture, and others were motivated to follow their artistic inclinations. Only Pollock could make Picasso's art look old!

It's intriguing to note that Pollock's artistic talent extended beyond the canvas and influenced popular culture. Both fans and detractors were drawn to his reckless ways and bohemian lifestyle. As his notoriety increased, Pollock found himself at the center of creative debate, questioning accepted wisdom and breaking convention.

Jackson Pollock blazed a trail through the annals of art history with his groundbreaking drip painting technique. That technique came about by study and incessant experimentation, leading to an innovation that every art appreciator benefits from.

Pablo Picasso

Whor it comes to artists who've fundamentally shaped the world of art, Pablo Picasso is undeniably in a league of his own. Indeed, Picasso didn't merely dip his toes into the art scene; he cannonballed into it, leaving ripples that continue to resonate through time.

Born in Spain in 1881, Picasso displayed a prodigious artistic talent from a young age. The youngster received formal art training from his father, a painter and art teacher. Yet Picasso's creativity refused to be constrained by traditional art education. He bore an insatiable curiosity and a ceaseless drive to navigate new artistic territories.

Picasso's voracious creative appetite led him through distinct stylistic periods: the melancholic Blue Period, the contemplative Rose Period, the African art-inspired Period, and finally into Cubism, the avant-garde style he co-founded with Georges Braque. Cubism shattered conventional perspectives, reconstructing objects and figures into geometric forms and offering multiple viewpoints simultaneously. This innovative approach revolutionized visual art, extending its influence to sculpture, literature, and even architecture.

Consider "Les Demoiselles d'Avignon," a painting that marks a radical shift in Picasso's style and the birth of Cubism. The painting's fractured depiction of five nude women was initially met with shock and disdain, but it ultimately heralded a new artistic epoch. Picasso, unperturbed by critics, continued to push boundaries and dismantle norms.

Just when the art world thought it had caught up with Picasso's revolutionary ideas, he shifted the paradigm again. This time, he turned to collage, incorporating unconventional materials like newspaper clippings and fabric into his artwork. This novel technique not only blurred the lines between high and low art but also introduced an entirely new visual language.

Despite Picasso's innovation, he was not an artist who discarded the past. Instead, he engaged with it, reinterpreting and transforming it. His series of 58 paintings based on Diego Velázquez's "Las Meninas" is a testament to this. He took an iconic work from the Spanish Golden Age and reimagined it through the prism of Cubism, thereby connecting historical art traditions with contemporary ones.

Picasso's influence can't be overstated. His relentless innovation inspired countless artists and continues to reverberate through the art world. His spirit of invention, his defiance of convention, and his ability to continually transform his art and the art world are why he is an 'Innovator' on the Cool Continuum.

Picasso once said, "I am always doing that which I cannot do, in order that I may learn how to do it." This constant drive to learn, to experiment, and to innovate was at the heart of Picasso's art. His extraordinary output — an estimated 50,000 artworks including paintings, drawings, sculptures, ceramics, prints, textiles, and rugs — acts as compelling evidence of his ceaseless artistic exploration.

In the landscape of art history, Pablo Picasso looms large, defining the terrain and influencing the climate around him. His life and work remind us that art thrives on experimentation and that the true Innovator is one who, like Picasso, is never content to rest but is always seeking the next horizon.

Puff Daddy

Puff Daddy (now primarily known as "Diddy") is one of the most successful rappers of all time, yet most people don't fully grasp the innovation he brought to the table. Puff Daddy, born Sean Combs, has brought a fresh perspective to the rap world and the music industry as a whole.

Combs quickly understood that to succeed, it was important to embrace the business side of music as well. For this reason, he started his own record label, Bad Boy Records, pretty early on. It was almost unthinkable to start an independent label in the late '80s, let alone a recording company with a focus on rap and R&B. In spite of all odds, Combs managed to break many chart-topping artists with an impressive collection of hits. Some of his signees include The Notorious B.I.G., Mase, and Mary J. Blige, artists who are still relevant to this day. Puff Daddy's savvy entrepreneurial spirit is why he stands out as an Innovator in the Cool Continuum.

Today, the relationship between hip-hop and business, "the hustle," is a very persistent trope of the genre, with many rappers glamorizing the business side of their music and trying to branch out with different enterprises. Puff Daddy helped pioneer this concept, influencing many generations of artists and musical entrepreneurs to come.

This wasn't the only rap trope that Puff Daddy popularized. He was one of the very first artists to create a connection between high-end fashion brands and the hip-hop community. The glamour, luxury, and excess associated with hip-hop have been influenced by Puff Daddy's ideas and his fondness for haute couture. To this day, fashion and hip-hop are deeply intertwined.

Puff Daddy's innovative approach wasn't just related to his business acumen. He was also a groundbreaking artist and producer in his own right. Most notably, Puff Daddy was one of the first producers to popularize the art of sampling and remixing in hip-hop and R&B music. Not only did he realize that artists could create some truly amazing songs this way, but he also realized that samples and remixes could be a great way to generate more income from a previously recorded piece of music by way of royalties and licensing for the parts to be sampled or remixed. This is a perfect example of how the rap mogul combined his talent with his entrepreneurial vision to create something new.

Some detractors argue that Puff Daddy's music lacks originality, as he heavily relied on samples and existing hits to create his tracks. However, he used samples and existing melodies as a canvas upon which he could paint a completely new picture. This gave way to a whole new approach to creating hip-hop, which is still extremely prominent to this day. Even modern artists like Juice WRLD or XXXTENTACION have embraced the style popularized by Puff Daddy during the heyday of the hip-hop golden age.

Puff Daddy also became one of the first artists to look for fans outside the hip-hop community. Once again, from a business perspective, he realized that he actually could appeal to a much broader market if he broke genre-specific barriers. In order to do that, he embarked on many collaborative projects involving artists from various genres, including rock and pop. By merging different musical styles, he broadened the reach of hip-hop and made it more accessible to new audiences. His innovative approach largely contributed to rap's mainstream status in culture.

The Ramones

Hailing from the street corners of Queens, NY, The Ramones are perhaps one of the most influential groups in modern music. Although they barely managed to scratch the surface in the mainstream music scene (and not for lack of trying), they became iconic in the alternative music world. Inspiring punk rock bands to come and, more importantly, reminding the world that simplicity can be an essential component in music, their influence is profound.

When the original members of the Ramones came together to form a band, they could barely play their instruments. Guitarist Johnny Ramone had learned a few chords from a Beatles songbook and tried his best to emulate the sound of the bands he looked up to, namely The Stooges and New York Dolls. Because of his limited vocabulary on the guitar, his sound was even more primal and rudimentary. Johnny auditioned for many local bands but was always rejected. He eventually found a home in The Ramones, which he formed with bassist Dee Dee, drummer

Tommy, and singer Joey, who was initially supposed to be the drummer.

The ramshackle group of young punks could be described as Outsiders in the Cool Continuum because they didn't think musicianship was a requirement to make music. Their formula was a resounding "1,2,3,4!" shouted by Dee Dee at the top of his lungs before diving into short yet melodic musical outbursts, often shorter than 3 minutes and never employing more than three chords. Despite their simplicity, the songs resonate with the punk community in New York City and elsewhere.

The Ramones made it to the UK, where they made an impression on the burgeoning local punk scene due to their fast live sets and dangerous image. Overall, The Ramones' fast and stripped-down punk rock style was revolutionary, laying the foundation for the entire punk movement several years before even The Sex Pistols were around. The band developed their signature sound from day one, and it was unlike anything heard before.

The Ramones spent so much time on the road that they perfected their own technique and became extremely proficient at the style they developed. To this day, even academically trained guitarists who have studied for decades struggle to play the all-downstrokes guitar technique favored by Johnny Ramone. Drummers, even the most experienced ones, can't always keep up with the fast one-handed sixteen-note beats required to perform most of the band's material.

Although the band started as a group of outsiders, they eventually shifted to becoming true Artisans in the Cool Continuum. The Ramones created a style from scratch, which is still considered the template of melodic punk rock music. Their style is often emulated, but the nuances and quirks in the band's sounds are seldom accurately replicated. Even in spite of several line-up changes throughout their tumultuous career, The Ramones stayed true to their sound. On one end, the group did not show much interest in evolving and experimenting with new ideas throughout its discography. On the other, The Ramones managed to build a very strong identity for themselves, almost like characters in a movie, which are always recognizable and easy to relate to.

Speaking of, the band was very aware of its image, and the members adopted matching leather jackets, ripped jeans, and shaggy haircuts, creating a cohesive and iconic image that reinforced their rebellious and anti-establishment ethos. They also used the "Ramone" surname for each member to create a sense of cohesion. This branding approach was a first in rock music, and it also showcases another side of the band's artisan outlook on punk music, expertly tailoring their aesthetic to match their vision.

Henry Rollins

The hardcore punk scene brewing in the USA during the mid-80s was certainly not an easy environment. From hostile audience members to cops, politicians, parents, and teachers, young punks had to fight off all sorts of outside forces looking to suppress their urgency and creative spirit. Many great bands came out of that scene, but nobody reached the legendary status of Black Flag. The California-based band was DIY to the bone. They built their gear, pressed their records, and even had their own record labels and booked their gigs. They were on a mission to carve their niche completely outside the music industry.

At some point, even the punk scene was restrictive to Black Flag, who set out to make increasingly more challenging, unpalatable music, even to punk audiences! The band always pushed it to the limits with their "us against the world" attitude. As one can imagine, being in such a contrarian and confrontational band was quite a challenge. For this reason, the band was a carousel of different members, always in and out of the group's revolving door. Between harsh touring conditions and no money, surviving as a member of Black Flag required enormous sacrifices and commitments. Many frontmen quit until Henry Rollins came along. He was the one person that had the anger, strength, and contentious spirit strong enough to match the band's crazy kaleidoscope of punk rock madness.

Henry Rollins, much like the rest of Black Flag, was "Outsider" right down to the molecule. He wasn't a musician but knew how to channel his rage through his gravelly vocals. Rollins is an Outsider in the Cool Continuum, but he is also considered an outsider among punks. Instead of looking like a "fashionable" punk star, Rollins adopted a very bare and minimalistic look, often wearing gym shorts and shaving his head. He was into health and fitness and didn't embrace drugs or alcohol, in sharp contrast with the rest of Black Flag and many fellow punk rockers.

Rollins was interested in the gnarliest, most hard-hitting alternative music out there, but he also had another side. He was interested in poetry and philosophy, and his influence led Black Flag to experiment with "Spoken Word." The band even recorded poetry-based albums, which, in perfect Black Flag style, enraged their punk rock audience! Eventually, the band imploded due to growing tensions between band members, but Rollins didn't stop. He started his own group, The Rollins Band, which enabled him to tour and experiment with rock music for two more decades. Eventually, he stopped focusing on music and became increasingly dedicated to his work as an author and speaker. He would travel the world on stand-up tours, not exactly as a comedian, but rather as a storyteller, often borrowing from his punk rock background and sharing many stories of traveling across the globe.

Throughout his career, Rollins has been an outspoken activist, advocating for various causes such as self-improvement, LGBTQ+ rights, animal rights, environmental preservation, and anti-war campaigns. He uses his platform as a force for change, inspiring people to take an active role in any change they wish to see in the world they live in. Punk rock taught Rollins that it is very important to be proactive and simply jump in to really make things happen. This exemplary life lesson is often at the core of his work, whether in his books or his former musical endeavors.

Bob Ross

Robert Norman Ross was no casual artist. His profound understanding of the wet-on-wet oil painting technique is proof of hardcore commitment and practice. His trademark landscapes, although not challenging artistic conventions, are testament to his ability to deliver technically proficient and aesthetically appealing works, the hallmarks of a Level 3 Artisan on the Cool Continuum. The tranquil meadows and mountains that grace his canvases did not occur by chance, but through a meticulous understanding of brushwork, color mixing, and paint behavior.

Being an Artisan isn't only about technical chops; it also involves recognizing one's strengths and limitations. Ross showcased this self-awareness in his approach to art education. Understanding that his art wasn't avant-garde, he instead focused on its potential to inspire. That's why he never tried to oversell the notion of mastering complex art styles like abstract impressionism or cubism. Instead, he stayed true to what he knew and believed his work could stir up the artist within everyone.

Ross's role as an art educator is critical to his placement on the Continuum. One might even argue that his real canvas was not the one he painted on, but the minds of his viewers. His true masterpiece was not a single painting, but the multitude of artists he inspired. He was brilliant at bringing out creativity in people who may have thought they could only stick to the norm. He didn't do this by showing off with complicated art concepts, but by guiding us toward simple, easy-to-understand ideas.

This brings us to another key aspect of the Artisan stage — influence. Ross's influence was not marked by a seismic shift in the world of fine arts. Instead, it was a gentle, nurturing influence. He played a pivotal role in making art accessible, pulling it down from the intimidating pedestal of elitism and placing it comfortably in our living rooms. Ross didn't start a revolution, but he sure inspired an evolution in the way we perceive art and our ability to create it.

Bob Ross's work personifies the Level 3 Artisan of the Cool Continuum. His technical proficiency, self-awareness, and consistent dedication — evidenced by his 31-season, 403-episode tenure on "The Joy of Painting" — cement his status in this category. If anything, Ross teaches us that the ability to inspire is an art form all its own.

Rush

Before the advent of progressive music, rock wasn't exactly considered a technically driven music style. Jazz drummer Buddy Rich was famously quoted as stating, "If you don't have the ability, you wind up playing in a rock band." The sentence was an example of the general attitude that "proper" musicians held in relation to rock'n'roll.

However, things took a different turn when Progressive hit the scene. The genre enabled musicians to expand on the energy of rock with influences from other styles. Incorporating elements of jazz, reggae, heavy metal, funk, classical music, and even ethnic music, prog-rock bands took the genre to new technical heights. Rush was one of the pioneers of the prog-rock revolution and one of the bands who made people realize that rock music could be challenging and technically stimulating.

Formed in 1968, this trio of virtuosic musicians, bassist-vocalist Geddy Lee, guitarist Alex Lifeson, and drummer Neil Peart, created a sound that defied the usual archetype of what a rock "power trio" could be all about. Record after record, Rush became synonymous with their unrivaled energy and technical skill, delivering mind-blowing performances (both live and in the studio) that elevated them to cult status.

Each member of Rush is technically gifted, having spent years mastering their respective instruments and the art of songwriting as a whole. For this reason, they fit within the Artisan level of the Cool Continuum. The band members brought an impressive level of sophistication to their songs. Rush is known for mastering odd time signatures, such as 7/8, 9/8, and 11/8. By contrast, most traditional rock music is in 4/4. Incorporating these non-traditional time signatures into their songs requires significant skills, not only as individual musicians but also as an ensemble.

Over the years, some naysayers have accused the band of "faking it" in the studio with the help of production trickery. However, Rush's live shows are evidence of their technical skill and actual abilities. Not only was Rush able to recreate their songs to perfection, but they also expanded on the studio version with extended improvised moments and impromptu instrumental sections, where the members had the opportunity to perform blazing solos.

Besides the music, the three personalities at the heart of the band made Rush special. The band members shared a unique and profound bond that extended far beyond their musical collaboration, so much so that the group stopped recording and touring due to drummer Neil Peart's health issues and his untimely passing. After over four decades of making music together, the original members felt there was no need to ruin the magic formula by dragging the band on. Rush became a symbol of sheer love of music and the joy of sharing the challenge of playing amazing riffs and complex parts, not to show off but to achieve a deeper goal together as bandmates and friends.

In doing so, they inspired and amazed many generations of musicians. As true rock artisans, Rush managed to introduce rock music fans to more challenging styles. Conversely, they also inspired jazz heads to give rock a shot since they showcased the most technically demanding side of the genre! Modern artists as diverse as Foo Fighters and Dream Theater have often cited Rush as a massive influence and stated that listening to the band when they were kids inspired them to play as well.

The "Holy Triumvirate" lives on in the memories of the fans and the surviving band members, who pay tribute to their fallen brother, Neil Peart, any chance they get.

Henri Rousseau

Some artists cultivate their skills within the structured gardens of prestigious academies, while others, like Henri Rousseau, let their creativity grow wild, fueled by passion and imagination. Operating outside the boundaries of traditional instruction, Rousseau represents an "Outsider" on the Cool Continuum.

Born in 1844, Rousseau spent most of his life as a toll collector in Paris, a job far removed from the glamorous world of art. It was only in his early 40s that he started painting seriously, making him a late entrant into the art world. What he lacked in formal training, Rousseau made up for with enthusiasm.

Rousseau's paintings radiate with creativity, unfiltered through the lens of academic instruction. His most celebrated works are dreamlike jungle scenes, alive with lush vegetation and exotic wildlife. One might imagine Rousseau as a well-traveled explorer, drawing from personal experiences in far-flung locales. Yet, the artist never ventured beyond

France. His jungles were products of his imagination, inspired by visits to botanical gardens and zoos, along with images from children's books and other publications.

Dubbed 'Le Douanier' (the customs officer) by the artistic community, Rousseau's style was often met with mockery. Critics scoffed at his lack of conventional perspective, his awkward anatomical renditions, and his flat, detailed depictions that seemed to ignore the established rules of Western painting. Yet, his works emanated a charm and vibrancy that the polished veneer of academic art often lacked.

Rousseau's paintings may not have had the complex sophistication of his professionally trained contemporaries, but it possessed a heartfelt honesty. He wielded his brush with an unpretentious directness that resonated with the public, offering a refreshing contrast to the elitism of the art world.

In time, Rousseau's artistic vision was recognized and respected by avant-garde artists such as Picasso and Kandinsky. His work inspired these artists to look beyond the confinements of conventional training, opening the door for modernist movements that would redefine the art world.

In the Cool Continuum, Rousseau's status as an 'Outsider' artist is a given. His path was unconventional, his technique untrained, and his vision untouched by the precepts of the academic art world. Despite never receiving formal art education,

Rousseau carved a niche for himself in the annals of art history.

It's through the raw, unfiltered lens of artists like Rousseau that we are reminded: art isn't solely the dominion of those with diplomas and refined tutelage. It also belongs to the dreamers who dare to listen to their heart and bring forth their own unique vision.

The Shaggs

The Shaggs, a sister trio from Fremont, New Hampshire, form a remarkable corner in the Level 1 'Outsider' stage of the Cool Continuum, the land of accidental prodigies and unconventional musicians. Like a wildflower sprouting in a meticulously manicured garden, their art bore a peculiar charm that took time to appreciate.

Formed in 1968 under the direction of their father, Austin Wiggin, the Shaggs consisted of sisters Dorothy, Betty, and Helen. Wiggin believed in a fortune teller's prophecy that his daughters would form a successful music band. However, he seemed to bypass the traditional route of music lessons, plunging the girls headfirst into public performances and recording sessions. The result was their debut album Philosophy of the World, a collection of 12 songs that sounded like nothing anyone had ever heard before.

The album was like a coloring book filled by a child who'd never seen the standard shades of the sky or grass — green might be pink, blue might be orange.

The guitar chords trembled as if walking a tightrope, the percussion staggered like a newborn deer, and the vocals were of a no frills discount variety. The sisters were like extraterrestrials trying to mimic Earth's music, creating a sound that was paradoxically alien and familiar.

While there is some semblance of musical ability hiding in the chaos, The Shaggs were not musicians proper; they were musical visitors. This isn't to say they were devoid of talent, but their talent wasn't on a wavelength that aligned with the commonly accepted frequency of musicality. They played their own version of rock 'n' roll, free from the shackles of rhythm, harmony, and melody.

Critics branded their music as discordant and untutored. Yet, in the discordance, there was an odd sense of unity. The unorthodox melody lines, off-beat drumming, and out-of-tune guitars came together like mismatched pieces of a puzzle, creating an entirely new picture, abstract but not without charm.

If music is a form of self-expression, the Shaggs expressed themselves in ways only they could. Their song lyrics ranged from reflections on daily life, like "My Pal Foot Foot", to profound philosophies of the world. The sincerity and directness in their words held a mirror to their honest approach to music, unfettered by pretense or conformity.

The Shaggs are the ultimate representation of the "Outsider" stage of the Cool Continuum. They may not have understood the nuances of chords or the rhythm's pulse, but they brought an unprecedented authenticity to their work. Their genuine, undiluted spirit places them in a category that overlooks technical finesse in favor of personal expression and individualistic creativity.

Frank Zappa once famously said that the Shaggs were "better than the Beatles". While this statement can be seen as tongue-in-cheek, it captures the essence of the Shaggs' appeal. They were not better in the traditional sense of musical skill; they were 'better' in their unapologetic departure from the norm, in their unfiltered creative expression, in their peculiar, audacious foray into the world of music.

The Shaggs were outsiders in a Top 40 industry, a technicolor polka-dot spectacle in a monochrome world. The imperfections in their music, the wobbly rhythm, and off-key harmonies were not defects; they were badges of their outsider status. They danced to their own beat, oblivious to the stringent metronome of the mainstream.

That's the captivating allure of the Shaggs, the quintessential outsiders in the grand continuum of creators, and they are considered iconic in music history.

George Strait

I t's a rare breed of artist who can steer a genre innovatively back to its roots. George Strait, the "King of Country," has led the charge in the world of country music. He's a different kind of 'Innovator' on the Cool Continuum. For Strait, innovation didn't mean breaking away from tradition, but returning to it, thereby creating a potent form of innovation within tradition.

George Strait's work has consistently evoked the essence of traditional country music while ushering in a fresh, invigorating interpretation of it. This was not about following the fads of the day; instead, he embraced the spirit of country music's past, thereby setting a course for its future.

In fact, one might say Strait's own last name seemed to serve as an omen. He kept country music on a 'strait' path, consistent with its roots, even when mainstream trends threatened to divert its course. It's as if his name was a calling, an innate responsibility to uphold the timeless tenets of country music.

Strait's pivotal album, "Strait Country," is credited with sparking the neotraditional movement in country music. His rich blend of hardcore honky tonk, Western swing, and the mellow strains of Bakersfield country captured the hearts of listeners. Even the softer ballads that filled the gaps between barroom anthems bore a traditional stance. AllMusic critic Stephen Thomas Erlewine observed that Strait's innovation was in showing "how it was possible to be planted firmly in traditional country yet flexible enough to play softer stuff without losing that hardcore stance."

Yet, innovation is only half the story. The Innovator category in the Cool Continuum also emphasizes influence. And George Strait's influence on country music is nothing short of profound. His insistence on traditional country sparked a new flame in the genre, one that continues to burn brightly today, igniting a renaissance of the genre's foundational sound.

Strait's career offers an insightful perspective on innovation. It reinforces that innovation doesn't always imply creating something entirely new; it can also mean reviving and reinterpreting the old. His influence in the country music scene acts as a steady foundation. Rather than eroding the genre's roots, his work reinforces them, keeping the music true to its authentic country origins.

In the Cool Continuum's spectrum, George Strait's work represents the "Innovator" stage, not because he broke from tradition, but because he returned to it in a fresh, captivating way. He created a powerful form of innovation within tradition, shaping the direction of country music, not by diverting its course, but by reaffirming it.

George Strait's legacy shows that true innovation can come from respecting and reviving tradition. His last name, Strait, becomes a powerful symbol of his role in country music — maintaining a straight, consistent path, keeping the genre true to its roots, even in the face of changing trends. Strait wasn't just a part of the country music current; he was the bedrock, channeling its flow back to tradition.

Cecil Taylor

Cecil Taylor was an influential jazz pianist, composer, and poet known for his innovative and avant-garde approach to music. Born on March 25, 1929, in New York City, he emerged as a prominent figure in the jazz scene during the 1950s and 1960s, pushing the limits of jazz and exploring new realms of improvisation and composition.

Taylor's musical style was characterized by unique and complex piano playing, marked by his virtuosic technique, percussive attack, and intricate rhythmic patterns. He often incorporated elements of free jazz, atonal music, and contemporary classical music into his compositions, creating a distinctive and groundbreaking sound. This sound grew, evolved, pushed boundaries, and ventured into places few have since been able to follow.

To fully understand why he should be regarded as a level 5 Genius on the Cool Continuum, it is through the evolution of his music across the albums he released that this progression from a 'one to watch' to someone who reached a jazz nirvana is best illustrated.

If his 1956 debut, 'Jazz Advance' (containing several interesting takes on genre standards) already hinted at an artist who was happy to experiment outside the fashions of the day, 'Looking Ahead' in 1958 delivered the breakaway from the usual Bebop traditions. The music became more ornate and intricate, and the songs became the perfect showcase for his powerful and percussive playing style.

In 1962, he released 'Nefertiti, The Beautiful One Has Come,' recorded live at the Cafe Montmartre in Copenhagen. Even today, it is regarded as an extraordinary live performance. Perhaps untethered by the conformities of the studio recording format, his interest in Free Jazz came to the fore through long, improvisational tracks built around speed, spontaneity, and complex musical conversations with his sidemen.

Unit Structures,' released in 1966, marks a milestone in his career, the title coming from a compositional concept that he now based his writing on — music following pre-determined parameters and lines but allowing room for improvisation and musical freedom. Such a musical template also allowed the sonic dialogues between him and his fellow players to be further explored, becoming an important focal point of his songs.

The same year, 'Conquistador!' also saw the light of day, an album that can truly be regarded as avant-garde and wonderfully adventurous in its approach. The title track itself, a nearly 20-minute exploration of complex rhythms and harmonies, showcases Taylor's innovative compositional approach and sets the tone for the rest of the album.

Seven years later, 'Indent' saw the light of day. This time, Taylor opted for a solo album. This more stripped-back format was a powerful demonstration of his unique style and individuality as an artist. His explorations of tone clusters, rapid-fire note sequences, and wide-ranging dynamics highlight his technical virtuosity and distinctive musical voice.

Two years later, 'The Cecil Taylor Unit' returned to a band format and featured a sextet, again allowing Taylor to display his skills when leading and interacting with larger groups. Here, his compositional structures became even more intricate, leading to densely packed sonic landscapes that further pushed the boundaries of jazz.

The next two decades gifted us one album each. 'For Olim' (1987), another solo album dedicated to a recently deceased friend, highlighted Taylor's ability to express deep emotion through his free jazz style. The improvisations are dense and complex, yet elegant, eloquent, and very personal and reflective. Finally, 'Tree of Life' (1994) shows that his innovation and experimentation remained undiminished even this far into an already musically adventurous and extraordinary career. The piano work contained on this album is as dense and powerful as ever, and his vision for where compositional free jazz and the broader jazz genre might go next is something he is still exploring with gusto.

Cecil Taylor should be regarded as a genius due to his groundbreaking contributions to jazz and music. His innovative approach to piano playing, incorporating free jazz and contemporary classical elements, showcased extraordinary virtuosity and redefined what jazz could be.

His compositions, displaying intricate structures and intense improvisations, have inspired future generations of avant-garde musicians, and his unique approach and exploration of language, sound, and rhythm extended to his poetry and scholarly work. Through his lifelong dedication to pushing artistic boundaries, Cecil Taylor left his unmistakable signature on jazz, solidifying his status as a true genre genius.

Quentin Tarantino

With no formal education in filmmaking, Quentin Tarantino blazed onto the movie scene with an irreverence that redefined Hollywood's storytelling norms. His background? Working at a video rental store. Yet, from this unlikely place, he emerged to revolutionize the filmmaking industry, placing him as a Level 2 "Rebel" on the Cool Continuum.

Tarantino's brand of cinema is a cinematic joyride that defies traditional storytelling norms. Like a jazz musician riffing through a standard, he takes familiar tropes and techniques and infuses them with his distinctive voice. His films, loaded with cultural references, intense dialogue, and graphic violence, unsettle, provoke, and captivate in equal measure.

His 1994 film, "Pulp Fiction," exemplifies this rebellious approach. It refuses to follow a linear timeline, jumping back and forth to unravel a darkly humorous narrative. Such an audacious, fragmented plot was seldom seen in mainstream cinema until

Tarantino made it his signature style. It's akin to tearing up a traditional novel and piecing it back together in a jigsaw puzzle that only he could create.

It would be hard to overstate Tarantino's influence. He has shaped the cinematic landscape with his audacious storytelling, prompting others to echo his style. Yet, while his impact hit Hollywood like a knuckle sandwich, it doesn't place him to a Level 4 "Innovator" on the Cool Continuum. His forte lies in reinterpreting and subverting established norms, not creating new ones.

The "Rebel" level on the Cool Continuum is not about lack of skills; it's about having the kahunas to twist those skills into something entirely unique. The classics of cinema are Tarantino's playground, a place where he toys with genre conventions, boldly remixes elements, and creates something exhilarating.

Tarantino's use of violence also signifies his rebellious stance. His films, from "Reservoir Dogs" to "Django Unchained," are notorious for their graphic scenes. But rather than using violence purely for shock value, Tarantino employs it to intensify the emotional beats of his narratives, and to comment on society's desensitization to real-world violence.

Then, there's his dialogue — Tarantino's characters often engage in lengthy, seemingly unrelated banter, diverging from the usual quick and purposeful movie dialogue. Yet, these dialogues fortify his characters with depth and humanity, and drive the narrative forward in a roundabout but riveting way.

Tarantino's stylistic rebellion extends to his eclectic choice of music. Ignoring the typical use of orchestral scores, he draws from a wide array of genres, creating unexpected yet strikingly effective combinations. Who could forget the unforgettable pairing of a gruesome ear-cutting scene with the cheerful 70s track "Stuck in the Middle with You" in "Reservoir Dogs"?

Even his filmmaking education is a rebellion of sorts. Rather than studying in a film school, Tarantino educated himself in the school of cinema by watching and analyzing movies during his time as a video store clerk. This unconventional path to filmmaking, unbounded by academic norms, surely fueled his disregard for Hollywood's status quo.

We can't reduce Tarantino to the simplistic labels of 'unskilled' or 'amateur'. His brash, viscerally striking style is a deliberate revolt against the ordinary — he knows the rules, but chooses to reinvent them. This is what Level 2 Rebels embody: a raw, passionate defiance that molds the industry to their will.

Quentin Tarantino's films have been like amphetamine to cinema's central nervous system. Certainly not everyone's speed, but his rebel spirit is precisely what defines a Level 2 "Rebel" on the Cool Continuum.

Minerva Teichert

Out in the wide-open fields of Wyoming, where the sound of horse hooves sets the daily pace, a different kind of beat emanates from Minerva Teichert's studio. Confronting the tough aspects of life on a ranch, raising five kids, maintaining activity in her Church and local community, and dealing with health issues from the paint she used, Teichert transformed her faith into massive, colorful murals.

Minerva Teichert, born in 1888, spent much of her life on a secluded ranch in Wyoming. Yet country living didn't confine her. She experienced a strong pull towards art and secured her formal education at the Art Institute of Chicago. This decision would shape her art style and profoundly impact how she approached her work. At the Institute, she was introduced to mural painting. She mastered this art form, turning expansive walls into visual stories of Jesus Christ and the Mormon pioneers crossing the plains, narrating tales as clearly as words on a page.

For Teichert, creating a mural wasn't solely about artistic expression, but also about teaching. Her staunch faith in the Church of Jesus Christ of Latter-Day Saints led her to perceive art as a means to educate and inspire others. Believing that the Church had the responsibility to save society through art, she imbued every brushstroke with thought, prayer, and a goal to spread the Restored Gospel.

She envisioned her murals as large, outdoor libraries, a fusion of color and shape that brought history and teachings to life for anyone who passed by. Her art wasn't merely about aesthetics; it was a tool for education, offering even a casual viewer a glimpse into the essence of a story. To Teichert, a mural functioned like a visual sermon, an art form aiming not only to decorate but also to teach, inspire, and kindle faith.

While her dedication to art remained steadfast, life presented its challenges. The very paint she used — laden with lead — jeopardized her health and vision. But Teichert never considered retiring her paintbrushes. Her art was her life calling, a commission from God. She was resolute in her determination to continue creating, despite the personal adversities she encountered.

Despite her strenuous work and involvement in civic activities, national recognition for Teichert's work was absent during her lifetime. She was an artist whose name, akin to the gentle whisper of the Wyoming wind, was predominantly unheard in the bustling art world of her time.

As we determine Teichert's position on the Cool Continuum, her commitment to craftsmanship, profound understanding of her medium, and her conviction in art as a pedagogical tool firmly place her in the "Artisan" category. She demonstrated the deep understanding and skill typical of a Level 3 artist and labored diligently to perfect her mural painting, thereby elevating the Saints and community she served.

Teichert's legacy persists as a potent influence in the art world. Back in Wyoming, amidst the steady rhythm of ranch life, her legacy endures — the "Artisan" whose murals became educators, the visual sermons, the vibrant reflections of a faith deeply intertwined with the narratives in her art.

Yun Hyong-keun

How does one create art? The question has sparked debates between those who attribute it to formal education and theoretical knowledge, and others who believe that true art arises from the soul. Within the realm of Korean artist Yun Hyong-keun, known for his minimalist and introspective paintings, an intriguing narrative unfolds. Let's dig into the facets of his unorthodox personality and artistic process, which define his artistic journey as he rejects the concepts and theories of academia. He's an exemplar of a Level 1 "Outsider" on the Cool Continuum.

While Yun's formal education in Western arts undoubtedly left an imprint on his artistic sensibilities, he later came to the realization that art cannot solely be an intellectual pursuit, nor its own paramount importance. Yun attached greater significance to human beings, society, and nature than to art itself. He understood that true artistic expression emanates from a realm beyond theory—a realm of awareness. Yun expressed this sentiment when he declared, "You can't make art from theory. I firmly believe that eternal and evocative art can only originate from a pure and untainted individual." This wisdom lies at the core of his organic and minimalist paintings.

This change in perspective likely stemmed from the hardships Yun endured in his early twenties. He was arrested, tortured, wounded, and expelled from school due to his involvement in campus-wide protests. However, his most trying times arrived a year later when the Korean War erupted. Because of his prior arrest, Yun was detained and even faced execution by a firing squad before miraculously escaping at the last moment. This transformative experience forever altered his outlook on art. No longer would he create art for art's sake, but rather as an expression of life itself. Gracefully retreating from the commotion of the art world, he sought solace in the serenity of his inner landscape. In this sacred space, he nurtured a deep connection with his creative source. Like a lotus emerging from muddy waters, Yun's artistic voice blossomed, untouched by external influences.

Yun Hyong-keun's artistic process unfolds as a transformative meditation in motion. With the stroke of his brush, he invites viewers to immerse themselves in a contemplative experience. His deliberate use of a limited palette, often restricted to burnt umber and ultramarine blue, mirrors the simplicity and purity of his artistic expression. Yet, despite such austere restrictions, his paintings emit an energy, an "invisible presence," a life force. Each brushstroke serves as a vessel, carrying profound emotions and insights that emerge from the depths of his being.

Yun Hyong-keun's commitment to authenticity and artistic purity offers a profound response to the timeless question of art's essence. Through his brushstrokes, we are reminded that art flows from the depths of the soul, unfettered by academia and societal conventions. His paintings reveal to us that art is a manifestation of life itself, like a journal entry celebrating another day he might not have had otherwise.

Banksy

Imagine this: One morning, you discover that a previously ordinary building in your city has become the canvas for a work of art, created by the enigmatic artist known as Banksy. This artwork appeared overnight, turning a mundane brick wall into a bold societal commentary, with stenciled figures challenging passersby with unflinching reflections of our world.

Emerging from Bristol's underground graffiti scene in the late 1990s to achieve international renown, Banksy exemplifies the concept of "out-of-nowhere innovation". His work, celebrated for its unique blend of artistry and activism, is widely studied.

The Level 4 Innovator of the Cool Continuum signifies artists who radically alter our perception of their medium, leaving a mark on the art world. These innovators, neither defined by their technical finesse nor their defiance of convention, drive their art into unknown territories, reshaping it from the ground up. Banksy, with his poignant social critiques immortalized in public spaces, decidedly tags this level as his territory.

Banksy's art doesn't reside in galleries or private collections; it unexpectedly surfaces in public spaces worldwide — from the West Bank barrier to the streets of New York City. His distinctive stenciled images, embedded with incisive socio-political commentary, weave into the everyday lives of people, prompting them to engage with often ignored issues.

Banksy's influence transcends his imagery. He has transformed the perception of street art from a stigmatized form to a respected medium of artistic expression. By challenging the traditional norms of the art world and expanding the limits of art's definition and location, Banksy has rendered art as a provocative and accessible part of the public landscape.

Consider 'Dismaland', a dystopian theme park installation in the UK conceived by Banksy in 2015. This was more than an artistic exhibit; it satirically critiqued consumer culture and the entertainment industry. The scale and ambition of this project underscore Banksy's innovative fire.

The air of mystery surrounding Banksy further solidifies his position as an Innovator. In an age obsessed with celebrity, Banksy's anonymity allows his art to do the talking. This unknown identity not only captivates public interest but also fuels broader discourse.

While it's straightforward to appreciate the ingenuity of Banksy's artwork, grokking its broader implications requires deeper contemplation. How does his rejection of artistic norms influence your understanding of art and its possibilities? Is the distinction between vandalism and art as clear-cut as once believed? These questions underscore Banksy's place on the Cool Continuum, and showcase art's capacity to innovate, challenge, and disrupt.

Jean-Michel Basquiat

Jean-Michel Basquiat. A name you see in art circles, a face framed by untamed hair that sears itself into memory. Yet, Basquiat and his work remain an enigma to many. Perhaps it's the brevity of his life, extinguished at a mere 27 years old, or the intricate fusion of visual languages — street art, poetry, low brow, high art, African motifs, and Western aesthetics — that defies easy categorization.

From a young age, Basquiat exhibited exceptional creativity. However, it was a car accident that became his turning point. Bedridden in a hospital, a copy of Gray's Anatomy, gifted by his mother, provided solace and forever influenced his art with an ultra-urban aesthetic that captivated audiences.

Peeling back the layers of the Basquiat mystery reveals his rise from the unforgiving streets as a graffiti artist under the alias SAMO©. The "Times Square Show" in 1980 catapulted him into prominence, where his art crackled with creativity, demanding attention and respect.

But why label Basquiat a Level 4 "Innovator" on the Cool Continuum? Innovators hone a distinct style and shatter conventional limits, redirecting the course of their field. Basquiat's legacy aligns with these qualities, confidently placing him in that category.

Unfettered by formal education, Basquiat emerged as a freewheeling dynamo of creativity. His works became intricate dances of text, symbols, and abstract figures, narrating tales of urban experience, racial inequity, and the human struggle. They were conversation starters for meaningful dialogue.

"Untitled" (1982) exemplifies Basquiat's impact — an auctioned piece with a haunting blue backdrop and a skull-like head that commanded a staggering $110.5 million in 2017. This fusion of African art, Abstract Expressionism, and graffiti encapsulated the urgency that permeated Basquiat's entire portfolio, reminding us of life's fragility.

Basquiat transcended his own creations, bridging the realms of high art and street culture. His influence rippled through the art community, shattering norms and expanding horizons for aspiring artists.

With his streetwise style and masterful amalgamation of visual languages, Basquiat redefined art, challenging conventional understanding. His innovations resonate through galleries and museums, slaking a thirst for modern multicultural paintings.

Acknowledging the gap between awareness and understanding, we trace Basquiat's journey from early inspiration sparked by a medical book to his fresh primal-urban aesthetic. Through the lens of the Cool Continuum, we now recognize Basquiat for what he was — an Innovator whose impact continues to reverberate through our collective memory.

Vivienne Westwood

T he only sin is to be boring," declared fashion mogul Karl Lagerfeld. Or maybe ChatGPT made that up, but it certainly sounds like something he'd say. Keeping this mantra in mind, one might argue that the inimitable Vivienne Westwood has led a life free of such artistic transgression. Her place in the annals of fashion history can be firmly categorized within the "Rebel" tier of the Cool Continuum, a ranking system acknowledging various stages of artistic development and impact.

Born in a rural Derbyshire village in England, Westwood's introduction to the world of fashion was far removed from the glamour and glitter of haute couture. She began as a primary school teacher who sewed her own clothes in her spare time, her designs mainly inspired by the fashion she saw in magazines. However, her life took a dramatic turn when she met Malcolm McLaren, the manager of the iconic punk rock band, the Sex Pistols. This fortuitous union ignited her transition from an obscure fashion enthusiast to a style icon.

It was the opening of the boutique 'SEX' on London's King's Road, a collaboration with McLaren, that catapulted Westwood into the public eye. The store became a hotbed for punk fashion, attracting attention with its radical designs that rejected convention and celebrated individuality. This marked her veritable springboard from obscurity, thrusting her into the spotlight and heralding the inception of her rule-bending reputation in the world of fashion.

Placing Westwood in the "Rebel" level of the Cool Continuum is a recognition of the spirit of rebellion that permeated her work and ethos. Her fashion philosophy took a sledgehammer to the establishment, smashing preconceived notions about what fashion should be. Each collection was an act of defiance, a statement that sartorial expression isn't defined by established norms but by the will and desire of the individual.

Her legacy is marked by her ability to challenge, disrupt, and provoke. From the brash punk aesthetic of her early career, complete with safety pins and padlocks, to the incorporation of British historical costumes and Savile Row craftsmanship in her later works, Westwood consistently rebelled against the status quo. She seemed to actively reject fashion trends, instead creating a parallel universe where her audacious vision ran rampant.

Just as an alchemist transforms base metals into gold, Westwood took the raw, aggressive energy of punk and refined it into high fashion. Her designs were not just clothes, but cultural commentary and political statements, echoing her socio-political views. She embodied the ethos of the 'Rebel', a maverick unfazed by public opinion, whose creations tore down the gilded gates of high fashion, democratizing it and offering it to the people in the streets.

Her influence is enduring, proving the power of rebellion in stimulating change. Vivienne Westwood continues to oppose the pervasive influence of social norms and market pressures. She embraced controversy and shunned complacency; her work often steeped in subversion, underlining the rebellious spirit that places her unapologetically in the 'Rebel' category of the Cool Continuum.

Vivienne Westwood stitched her garments together with daring cuts, provocative themes, and a fiery passion for change. As such, she is not merely a fashion designer, but a rebel with a cause, crafting a world where defiance reigns supreme, and where art — far from being boring—becomes an instrument of change.

Hunter S. Thompson

Every artist knows what it's like to fight for attention, kind of like a small plant under a big tree, trying to reach the sun. The problem you're probably dealing with right now is how to get noticed in the crowded world of art. One guy who figured this out was Hunter S. Thompson. Renowned for his work in the "gonzo" journalism style, a writing method that blurs the lines between fiction and non-fiction and puts the journalist at the center of the story, he's what you'd call a "Rebel" on the Cool Continuum.

Thompson was a real character who always went his own way. A writer by trade, he served a difficult apprenticeship in journalism, cutting his teeth on sports reportage for a small-town newspaper following his stint in the Air Force. A true rebel, he chafed at the conventional bounds of his early career, repeatedly bumped up against the law, and developed a reputation for heavy drinking and drug use, which became integral aspects of his public persona.

He was also famous for his flamboyant and chaotic lifestyle, reflected in his writing. Thompson's notorious "Fear and Loathing on the Campaign Trail '72", a collection of articles covering the 1972 presidential election, demonstrated his disregard for journalistic objectivity. His vivid, emotional, and often chaotic portrayals of the political landscape were a far cry from traditional objective reportage.

Thompson's breakthrough came after he decided to spend a year with the dangerous Hell's Angels motorcycle gang and wrote a book about it. This bold move made him famous and proved he was a true rebel. However, his best-known work, "Fear and Loathing in Las Vegas", is a perfect example of his rebellious nature. The book, a blend of fact and fiction, breaks many of the accepted conventions of writing and journalism, and reveals Thompson's deep-seated contempt for authority.

Moreover, Thompson was one of the first to criticize the 'American Dream', and his work often illustrated the divide between American ideals and reality. His prose throbbed with an urgency that laid bare the disillusionment of his generation. His work wasn't just about being a rebel, it was about showing the flaws and hypocrisy in society.

"As things stand now, I am going to be a writer. I'm not sure that I'm going to be a good one or even a self-supporting one, but until the dark thumb of fate presses me to the dust and says 'you are nothing', I will be a writer." Such was Thompson's resolve during his struggling days. Frustration, uncertainty, and feeling stuck were not enough to deter him from his chosen path.

Thompson showed that the hard times can be what fuels your work. He didn't just watch life; he lived it, and it showed in his prose. His stories were real and exciting because he was there, experiencing it all. Risking it all. He not only observed the world but also immersed himself in it, often becoming a central character in his own stories.

In the same way, your struggle could be the spark that gets your art going. Thompson wasn't just a rebel for the sake of being a rebel. Rather, his rebellion helped him present unfiltered experiences to the world. The lesson here is that being a rebel isn't the goal; the goal is to put your real self into your art.

"Buy the ticket, take the ride" Thompson used to say. The ride was fraught with challenges, but the rewards, as he found, could be great. Courage and authenticity, as Thompson's life demonstrates, can guide you to the recognition you yearn for.

In a world full of artificiality, will you let your real self show in your work? This is what you should be thinking about. It's not about following a set path; it's about carving your own through the wilderness of content. Thompson may not be a role model for you, and that's okay, but he leaves behind clues to success. Your creative path is up to you. That little plant can reach the sunlight. It just needs the light of real authenticity.

Johannes Vermeer

Johannes Vermeer, a luminary of the 17th-century Dutch Golden Age, was a painter who didn't change art through innovation, but refined it, creating an unerasable mark of genius. Vermeer, by this measure, occupies the fifth level on the Cool Continuum — a space for the rarefied and extraordinary.

Vermeer's stellar output may be due to his involvement within a vibrant community of painters. They often exchanged techniques, dabbled in overlapping themes, and shared studio spaces, fostering an environment rich in collaboration and inspiration. Vermeer's membership in the Guild of Saint Luke in Delft, a haven for painters and various artists, was particularly influential. This guild granted him invaluable opportunities to engage with his contemporaries, serving as the foundation for his development. This camaraderie and the guild's mentorship shaped Vermeer, allowing him to hone his craft to the genius level he later achieved.

The Level 5 Genius involves transcending traditional techniques and concepts, embodying an artistry that becomes as intuitive as it is unique. It's the realm of an artist who creates a body of work so profound that it alters our perception of the world. Vermeer's depictions of domestic scenes do just that, serving as a window into a tranquil universe that captivates us with its serenity and stillness.

Vermeer's genius is like a maestro who doesn't compose a new symphony but performs an existing one with such exceptional virtuosity that it forever changes how we listen to it. His understanding of light and color, his painstaking attention to detail, and his ability to infuse ordinary scenes with luminosity have rarely been matched. In "Girl with a Pearl Earring" or "The Milkmaid", Vermeer transformed everyday scenarios into something sublime, leading us through an intimate narrative filled with suspense and revelation.

One might argue that Vermeer, using an optical aid as suggested by Tim Jenison's theory, disqualifies him as a Level 5 Genius and instead plants him firmly as a Level 3 Artisan. An Artisan, in the Cool Continuum, demonstrates a solid grasp of techniques, consciously aware of abilities and limitations. They create aesthetically pleasing, technically proficient works. Yet, even if we accept the possibility of Vermeer using optics, it doesn't designate him to the artisan's realm.

Jenison's theory that Vermeer used a camera obscura or similar device is compelling. The optical tool could project an image onto a surface, guiding an artist to replicate scenes with photographic precision. Jenison, not an artist by trade, managed to recreate a Vermeer painting through this process, offering an intriguing method to explain Vermeer's virtuosity. But this technique does not account for Vermeer's creative genius or his remarkable sense of composition.

Think of it this way: a typewriter alone does not make a novelist, nor does a well-tuned piano create a pianist. These are tools, and it's the skilled hands and minds that manipulate them into something beyond the ordinary. Similarly, even if Vermeer used an optical aid, it doesn't diminish his genius. The device doesn't choose the right mix of pigments or compose a scene rich with narrative subtlety and emotion; the artist does. It is Vermeer's talent to breathe life into static domesticity and his remarkable ability to make silence speak volumes, which land him in Level 5.

In Vermeer's work, we witness not just technical excellence but a depth of understanding and feeling that transcends the mundane, making the everyday seem extraordinary. This profound intimacy with his subject matter and its delicate, almost tender rendering on the canvas is what separates Vermeer from the artisans. It's why he belongs at the center of the Cool Continuum.

Beyoncé

Beyoncé's emergence as an Artisan on the Cool Continuum began in her early days as the lead vocalist of Destiny's Child, one of the best-selling girl groups of all time. This established a solid foundation for her, setting the course for a career that would impact the universe of music and performance.

In this context, the term 'Artisan' is not merely about technical proficiency but underscores an artist's tireless ambition to perfect their craft and consistently raise the bar. This is Beyoncé — the artist where instinct and precision unite with sound and movement.

Each of Beyoncé's albums serves as a marker in her timeline, a bold foray into new musical territories while preserving the unique Beyoncé touch. Her self-titled album and the visually stunning "Lemonade" expand the possibilities of what an album can be, seamlessly blending audio and visual elements to create holistic artistic experiences.

In a world of fleeting trends, Beyoncé's commitment to her craft is impressive. Much like an artisan transforming raw material into something extraordinary, she pours her soul into each project. The result is a discography that attests to her relentless pursuit of artistic perfection and performances.

Beyond music, Beyoncé's talent as a performer — an elaborate ballet of choreography, stage presence, and audience connection — further demonstrates her artisanship. Watching Beyoncé perform is to observe a seasoned artisan at work, with every movement precise and meaningful.

An essential trait of the Artisan is the ability to channel emotion through their craft. Beyoncé's music is cathartic, personal, and relatable, fostering an intimate connection with her audience that blurs the line between performer and listener.

From her start with Destiny's Child to her spectacular solo career, Beyoncé has steadily honed her artistry, perpetually refining and augmenting her repertoire. She continues to set new benchmarks in the music industry.

Echoing Beyoncé's own words, "I don't like to gamble, but if there's one thing I'm willing to bet on, it's myself." In the high-stakes realm of musical artistry, Beyoncé's wager has indeed paid off.

Gibbons Twins

For some, the act of creation is more than artistic expression; it's a lifeline. This was true for June and Jennifer Gibbons, the "Silent Twins," who were born in Barbados but raised in Wales. They not only wrote stories but also lived in a world of their own making. When we look at their work and lives using the 'Cool Continuum', we can confidently say these twins were Level 1 "Outsiders".

The term "Outsider" conjures up images of those who are against the odds and on the fringes. This description aptly fits the Gibbons twins. Known for their elective mutism, they communicated with each other in a language all their own, withdrawing from society into a world crafted from their dreams and nightmares.

These twin authors had no traditional literary training to lean on. Their creativity grew while they lived on their own, often waging psychic warfare against each other. They wrote with raw emotion, creating works that were unrefined yet intense, a direct reflection of their lives. This lack of formality in their writings, an echo of their secluded existence, plants them deep inside "Outsider" territory.

The stories written by the Gibbons twins weren't popular during their lifetimes and likely never will be. This isn't conventional stuff. Take, for instance, June Gibbons' novel, "The Pepsi-Cola Addict." Freshly republished and available on Amazon, it reveals the life of Preston Wildey King, embroiled in scandal, reform school, and addiction. The storyline takes dramatic twists, mirroring the quirky imagination of its author. It's a universe away from familiar storytelling patterns, but it definitely resonates with the Outsider spirit.

However, being an Outsider on the Cool Continuum doesn't mean they aren't important to literature. The twins' unpublished works, a jigsaw puzzle of manuscripts and diary entries, offer us a stark view of their interiority. They reveal how hard it was to be twins, yet to be so suspicious of each other, and how much they wanted to connect in a normal, healthy way with their family and society at large. Yet, they did not succeed.

As the Cool Continuum suggests, creativity isn't about reaching a goal. Instead, it's about continuous expression regardless of the medium. Despite their personal turmoil and hardships, June and Jennifer Gibbons managed to leave a significant imprint on the world. Their lives inspired a song by the Manic Street Preachers, a best-selling book, numerous plays, two operas, and two documentary adaptations.

And now, with "The Pepsi-Cola Addict" back on shelves, the outsider narrative becomes more compelling. It beckons us to ponder the definition of art and an artist's life. The Silent Twins' lives and work remind us that the ways of making art are vast and diverse, teeming with stories that await an audience. Their silent voices raise a fundamental question: Are we ready to embrace unexplored territories of creativity? This, dear reader, is a thought for you to mull over.

Sid Vicious

In equal parts idolized and reviled, Sid Vicious is one of the most controversial figures in music. Many decades later, his influence still lives on, as he established his mark as the archetypal Outsider in The Cool Continuum and in music.

Born John Simon Ritchie, Vicious was a British musician and a prominent figure in the punk rock movement. He was not a musician in the traditional sense at all. Still, he was asked to replace the original bass player in the band Sex Pistols almost exclusively for "branding" purposes. He had the attitude and look that the band's manager, Malcolm McLaren, was looking for. Vicious didn't contribute to most recordings in the relatively minute discography of the band that made him famous. On many occasions, his bass wasn't even turned on during live performances, as he was often too wasted to play or not in tune.

While this outsider had musical skills comparable to an absolute beginner, he brought much more to the table. The punk culture was characterized by rejecting mainstream norms and embracing individuality, so musicianship was not the most paramount concern for people in the punk community. Sid Vicious wasn't a poser trying to look like a shocking punk rocker. He embodied the self-destructive, no-care attitude that made punk feel so exciting and dangerous. Even if he couldn't play very well, Sid Vicious brought an unmatched raw energy to his performances on stage, introducing an element of danger to Sex Pistols' live shows.

Eventually, the Sex Pistols imploded, with growing tensions among the band members and their management. Following the band's demise in 1978, Vicious attempted a brief and tumultuous solo career. He managed to record a few songs, including a cover of Frank Sinatra's "My Way." The song, often seen as a parody of the original classic, was so much more than that. It was a powerful symbol of a newer generation of musicians rejecting a previous generation's stiff rules and restrictions. While the Sinatra classic is impressive for the singer's vocal skills and orchestral arrangement, Vicious made a version that threw up on all the "perfection" of the original, highlighting all the imperfections and wearing them proudly. This cover is often cited as an example of the punk ethos. It's all about embracing individuality and using music as a way of self-expression rather than trying to create something with commercial or artistic value.

Unfortunately, Sid Vicious never had the opportunity to release a full-fledged solo album. Sid's unpredictable and controversial behavior contributed to his image and storied reputation, but it ultimately proved fatal. He was known for his onstage antics and aggressive attitude, which often led him to fights with other musicians, cops, and bystanders alike. These antics also led to a series of murky circumstances, which would ultimately cause the musician's death.

Sid Vicious tragically passed away at a young age due to a drug overdose at 21 years old, after his involvement with the death of his then-girlfriend Nancy Spungen. It is still unclear whether Sid Vicious killed Nancy or whether the two were victims of a robbery in their NYC hotel room. Still, the incident had a huge emotional impact on Vicious, who died shortly after that. To this day, the story of "Sid and Nancy" symbolizes the destructive allure of fame and its darker side. In addition, it is often seen as an example of the consequences of drug addiction and self-destructiveness, especially in relation to becoming very famous at a young age.

His untimely death and persona immortalized him as an icon in punk history and in rock music. The mystique surrounding his life and the impact of his music solidified his status as an outsider even after his passing.

About the Author

J ason S. Comely is an interdisciplinary artist and author of several books. He is the creator of the self-help game Rejection Therapy, the Tuduka Method, and Critical Stimulus. A proud father of three daughters, Jason describes himself as a Level 1 Outsider on the Cool Continuum. Explore more at jasoncomely.com. For inquiries or conversation, he can be reached at jason@continuum.cool.

www.ingramcontent.com/pod-product-compliance
Lightning Source LLC
Chambersburg PA
CBHW072155290526
45794CB00004B/1523